BACH to ROCK

an Introduction to Famous Composers and their music

I LOVE TO ROCK

with related activities

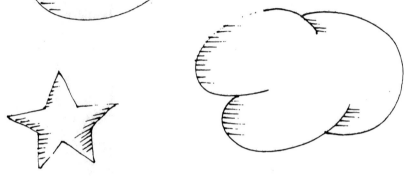

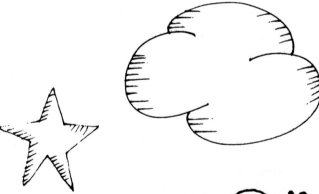

ISBN: 0-9621952-0-0

Additional copies may be ordered from:

THE ROSEMARY CORP.
P.O. Box 15572
New Orleans, LA 70175
Tel: (504) 895-4247

Also available:

A ninety-minute **BACH TO ROCK** audio cassette with 32 excerpts from musical compositions recommended by the text, and a **BACH TO ROCK** video.

LETTER TO THE READERS

When I began this book I had no conception of what a real job was ahead for me. Even though the idea had been in my mind for several years, the thought of putting down on paper a few facts about men and their music did not seem so formidable. However, once I had begun, the picture changed rapidly. First came the very perplexing decision of which composers would be the most representative to include. Next, after selecting the "men" came the problem of choosing representative works which would also be appealing to young listeners. I am quite sure that in my selections I have left out composers whom many readers will feel were terrible omissions, but because of not wanting an introductory book to be too long I had to limit my choices.

Goodness only knows how many years this might have taken had we depended upon me for typing! I can not say enough thank-you's to Elinor Woitha who tirelessly and, ostensibly, cheerfully typed, re-typed and re-typed the retypes!!

I have three teacher friends, Sheila Schwarzmann, Betsy McCutcheon and guitarist Richard Greene, who graciously gave of their time to read the text for content and mechanics.

Mr. Tom Wafer, Louisiana State Supervisor of Music Education, Mrs. Lorraine Wilson, Orleans Parish Music Supervisor, and Dr. Ed Kvet, acting assistant Dean of Loyola College of Music, gave me invaluable help and encouragement. One of my oldest friends, Carolyn McLellan, a writer-producer, guided me initially, but she gave me the greatest gift imaginable, an introduction to Mary Sue Roniger who became my instant illustrator. As I progressed with the text, her whimsical drawings added their special touch to the book, and her children, Peter and Sarah, were helpful critics for both drawings and text.

My father, Ted Gugert, provided me with the very necessary financial assistance, our good friend Henry Flower has "listened" with a critical and helpful ear and my attorneys, Esmond Phelps and Robert Walmsley, have tried to protect me so carefully. All have helped nurture this project and receive my heartfelt thanks.

But most of all how I have appreciated the love and patience and encouragement and good-humor of my husband Kenneth and three children, Wendy, Teddy, and Ken. They have put up with a totally cluttered dining-room table, the many "I can't do's" because of the book, my crossness when frustration set in, or my idiotic exhilaration when I felt I had hit upon a super idea. They have been wonderful.

Now it is finished, the writing stage, and all the time and work invested in BACH TO ROCK have been most rewarding. After less than a year the greatest prize I might have hoped for - opening the door to the world of music - has been achieved. The book has found itself in many elementary and secondary schools as well as in colleges (for teacher preparedness) and even in such prestigious places as the Historic New Orleans Collection and the Metropolitan Museum in New York. With all of this exposure and hopefully more, the numerous pleasures and hours of happiness of music will be enjoyed by an even wider and more varied audience.

Foreword - To Teachers

It is my sincere wish that this young people's introduction to composers and their music will promote an interest in and an awareness of the beauty and pleasure of music. I have tried to select representative artists of each period, and to make them "come alive" by telling a pertinent fact or two about each one's life and works. I realize that many schools may have a limited record or tape collection, so I have added, at the end, additional selections of music for listening. However, any music which you have on hand by the particular composer being studied will certainly be acceptable. I have also tried to choose examples which I feel would be geared to a basic introductory level.

Having taught music in schools both to younger students and high school seniors I have found that active participation in a subject helps to serve as a stimulant. Therefore, Mrs. Roniger and I have endeavored to create activities (which pertain to the particular composer and his works) for the student's use as a motivating exercise and a learning tool as well. Each teacher knows his or her students and their capabilities and in all probability will have additional ideas for activities or projects which may even tie in with another subject. If so, by all means use them. Our suggestions need only serve as guides. There are numerous ways for students to broaden their active involvement in music. Charades (acting out titles of compositions or composers names); reading additional material about a composer and giving a written or oral report on their finding; reading about other composers in the periods discussed but who are not mentioned in the book are all possible activities. A group activity might be to make a mural with a time-line beginning with 1600 (The Baroque) and to put all sorts of things on it (with the composers as the center) such as historical, political, scientific, art, etc. facts. Still another could be a spelling bee with teams, using musical terms, composers, works, etc. and telling one fact about each one.

The list of involvements is endless. We have provided suggested activities at the end of each section as well as summary activities relating to each period.

The glossary contains all bold faced words encountered in the text. Some are defined within the text paragraph, while others are foot-noted. When a definition seemed to interrupt the flow of the text, the latter (foot-noting) was chosen.

FOREWORD

A few years ago as a teacher, I had the pleasurable task of "putting together" a course, classified under the rather forboding title, The History of Music. It was to be taught to a group of seniors in an all-girls school. This was quite a challenge, one which has culminated in the "putting together" of this book.

Once during class I happened to mention Mendelssohn, and one of the students giggled and asked if Mendelssohn was a new dish on Brennan's menu, a local restaurant. I was **appalled!** Here was a classroom full of eighteen year old girls, from backgrounds and families with exposure to all of the arts, and yet their knowledge of music and composers was totally lacking. This really disturbed me, as music has always been a great source of pleasure to me. I began to think of some way in which I could introduce young people, boys and girls, to the richness and beauty of music and the people who created it.

I have found from experience, both as a classroom teacher and as a piano instructor, that if you wait too late to awaken an interest in music you may lose an avid fan altogether. The best time, I believe, to develop an awareness of who the composers are and the music which they have written is in the very early grades. The younger people have not yet closed their minds to "all that hi-brow stuff," and are eager to learn new things – especially if the material is introduced in an attractive way, with activities to go along with it. Hence – *Bach to Rock, a Rainbow of Composers.*

I hope that the writings in this book plus the suggested works to listen to will help to open a whole new world to young people – a world which can bring them much joy and happiness throughout their lives – when alone as well as with others.

Hi! I'm St. Cecilia, Patron Saint of Music. Come discover our rainbow of musical riches! Let's go!

Table of Contents

1.   Music
2.   Where
4.   When
5.   What
6.   Who
7.   Periods We'll Study

8.   Baroque Composers
         Johann Sebastian Bach
         George Frederick Handel
         Activities

18. Classical Composers
         Joseph Haydn
         Wolfgang Amadeus Mozart
         Activities

28. Romantic Composers
         Ludwig van Beethoven
         Franz Schubert
         Hector Berlioz
         Felix Mendelssohn
         Frederick Chopin
         Robert Schumann
         Franz Liszt
         Johannes Brahms
         Activities

50. Nationalistic Composers
         Giusseppi Verdi
         Richard Wagner
         Johann Strauss Jr.
         Peter Tchaikovsky
         Nicholas Rimsky-Korsakov
         Edward Grieg
         Jean Sibelius
         Sir Arthur Sullivan
         Edward Elgar
         Activities

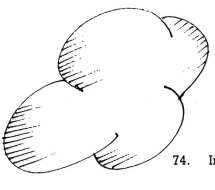
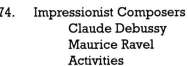

74. Impressionist Composers
 Claude Debussy
 Maurice Ravel
 Activities

84. Modern Composers
 Sergei Prokofiev
 Igor Stravinsky
 Activities

94. Ragtime, Blues, and Jazz
 Scott Joplin
 W.C. Handy
 Louis Armstrong
 Activities

106. American Composers
 Stephen Foster
 John Philip Sousa
 Irving Berlin
 George Gershwin
 Aaron Copland
 Richard Rogers
 Activities

124. Mid Century Composers
 Leonard Bernstein
 The Beatles

132. What Next?
135. The Orchestra
139. Appendices
 Glossary
 Suggested Listening
 Index

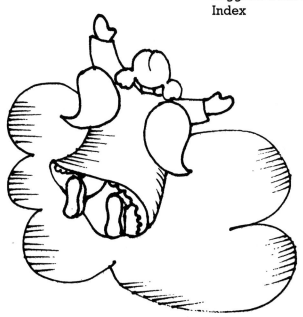

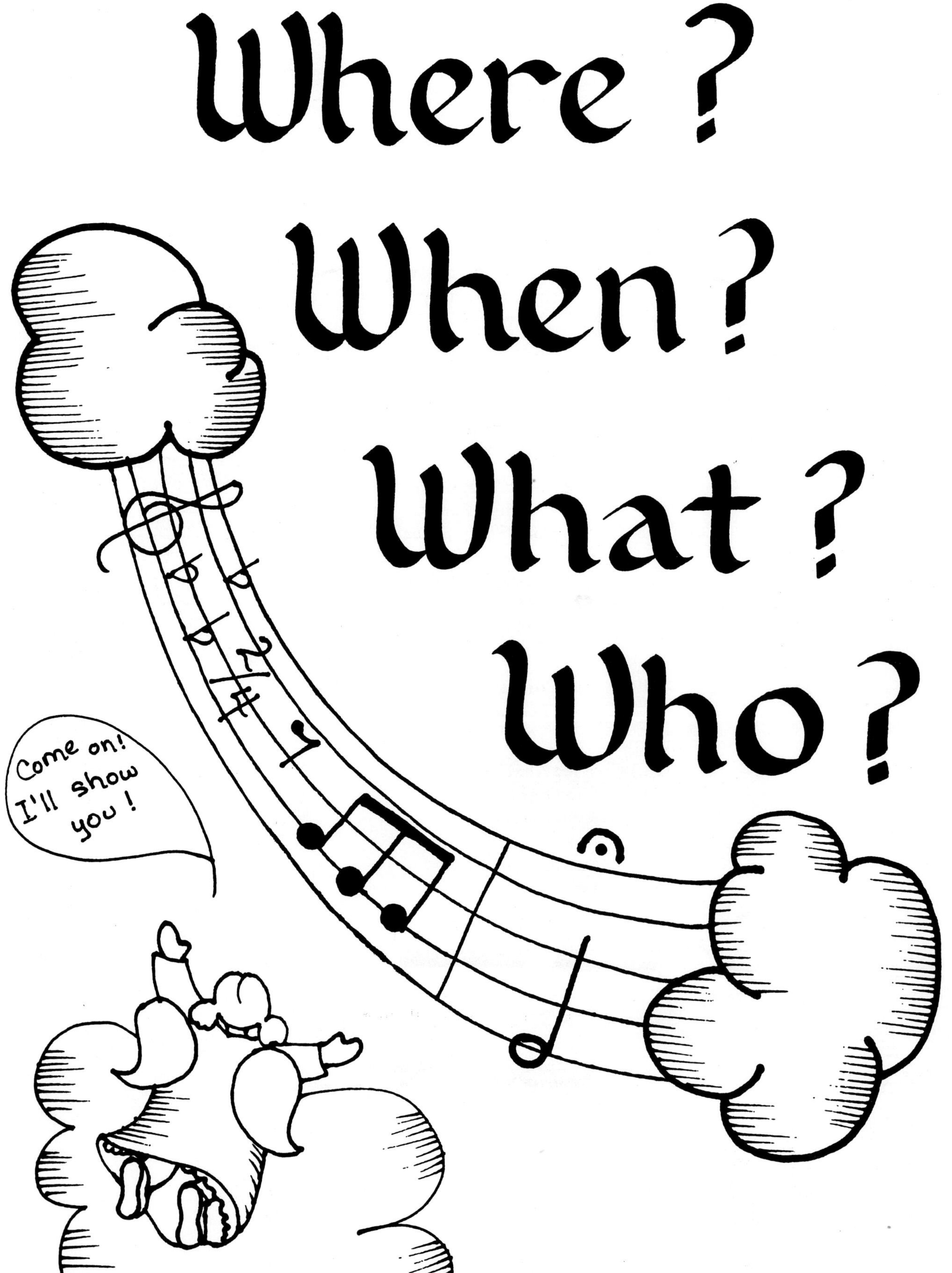
Where?
When?
What?
Who?
Come on! I'll show you!

Music...

WHERE?

Music is all around us. Almost every place we go we hear music. When we are in the dentist's office music is played in the background. When we go shopping, we hear music in the stores. Can you imagine how quiet and dull a parade would be without bands playing and drums beating? Who ever heard of a circus without music being played for the Grand March and all the performers' acts? When we get into our car, we turn on our radio to listen for our favorite song. We sing hymns in church, and we sing our National Anthem at the football games. Can you think of some other places where we hear music? See if you can draw pictures of some places or write the names of some places where music is played.

Can you draw a scene where you hear music?

WHEN?

Music has been around since man's earliest days. Long, long ago when people still lived in caves, they heard a kind of music in nature. Birds sang, wind whistled, and oceans roared. The cavemen struck wooden sticks and blocks together to send messages. The natives of Africa had special chants or songs to be used for healing sick people. The American Indian had special songs and dances used in asking for rain. Gradually, over many thousands of years, songs and chants have been used in daily life — for planting crops — for hunting and fishing — for weddings — for all sorts of celebrations.

Most of the early music of Europe which was written down was used for church services. Later, about 1600 in Europe, more and more music was written for dancing, or partying or for kings and princes in their courts. These composers are the people we shall meet in our book.

WHAT?

What is Music? Music is sound. It can be loud, it can be soft. It can be happy or it can be sad. It can be high, it can be low. It can be sung or it can be played on an instrument.

Music is rhythm. Rhythm makes music move. It can be fast, it can be slow. It can be jumpy or it can be smooth.

Music has melody. A melody is a tune that can be sung or whistled or hummed.

There are all types of music. There is serious music which we call symphonic. There is musical theater in which people talk and sing and act. There is ballet, which is a story danced to music. There is opera, which is a play told only in music by singers. There is popular music sung by rock and roll groups like the Beatles. There is country music, folk music, jazz music, bluegrass and others. Can you think of anyone who is a country music singer? Can you think of anyone who is a jazz musician? Also, can you think of any other kind of music or musician?

COUNTRY MUSIC SINGER

JAZZ PERFORMER

OTHER KINDS OF MUSIC

WHO?

So many kinds of music! But do you know who wrote any of this music? Do you know the names of any of the composers or anything about them? Do you know the names of any of their compositions? We can't introduce you to all the important composers, but in this book you will meet some of them and learn something about their lives. Also, we shall suggest some of their wonderful music which we hope you will enjoy hearing.

Periods We'll Study

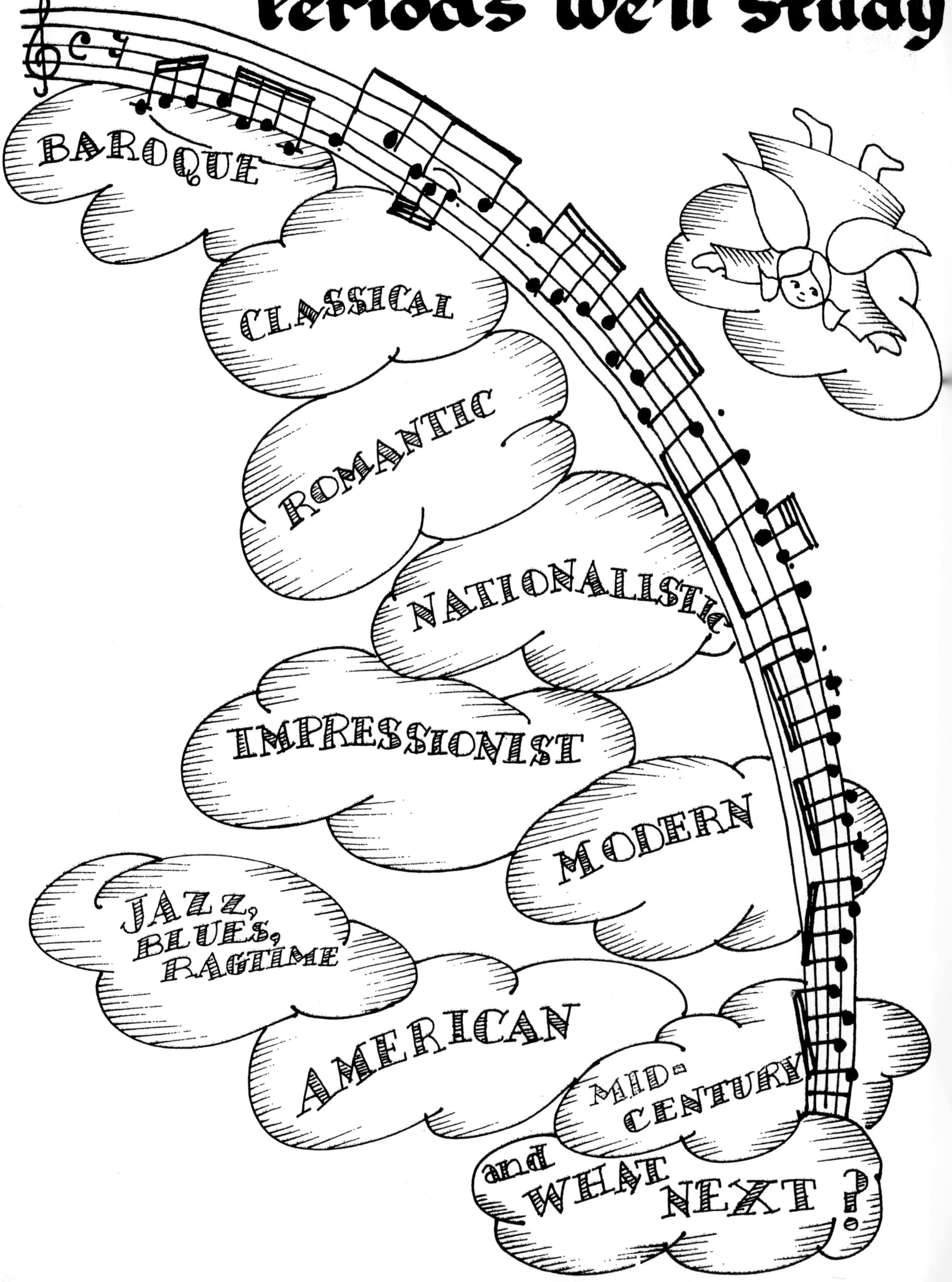

BAROQUE

CLASSICAL

ROMANTIC

NATIONALISTIC

IMPRESSIONIST

MODERN

JAZZ, BLUES, RAGTIME

AMERICAN

MID-CENTURY

and WHAT NEXT?

Baroque Composers

Bach

Handel

and other people
of their time:

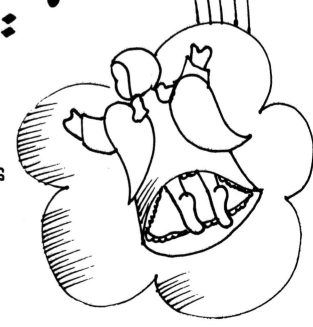

Louis XIV, the Sun King,
was King of France.

Isaac Newton made advances
in science and mathematics.

The Pilgrims were busy
settling America.

Rembrandt van Rijn was
painting his famous pictures.

Baroque

The story of music is divided into sections or periods. Each one has its own name and its own personality. The first period we shall read about is called the **Baroque.** Isn't that a funny sounding word? It just means a very fancy, decorated style of music and painting and building that was popular in Europe from about 1600 until 1750. While all this elaborate art and music was being developed in Europe, the Pilgrims had just come to America to build their first, simple homes and to celebrate their first Thanksgiving.

A new kind of music began during this dramatic period. It was called **opera.** An opera is a story or play set to music. We shall study more about opera later in our book.

Two great composers of this Baroque Era are Johann Sebastian Bach and George Frederick Handel. Bach wrote in all forms of music except opera and composed music especially for the organ and the church. Handel composed music for the opera as well as the other forms of the day. He also composed the famous Christmas carol, "Joy to the World."

Suggested Listening: Let's listen to the "Hallelujah Chorus" from Handel's oratorio, **Messiah.** This is a familiar example of the great music of Handel.

the Organ

During the Baroque period the organ was very popular, and much music was written for it, especially by Bach. It was used mainly in churches to perform sacred (religious) music.

How many of you sing hymns when you go to church? Have you ever wondered about the great big instrument, the organ, that often accompanies the church singing? It has dozens of sets of pipes through which air is blown to produce sound. In earlier times, the air was pumped through the pipes by means of a hand or foot-operated bellows. If the organ was large, it often took several people to operate the bellows while the organist played on the keys. Can you imagine what a difficult job that must have been! Modern organs are equipped with an electrical machine for supplying air to the pipes.

Some organs have several keyboards (manuals) played with the hands, and one played with the feet called the pedal keyboard. There are stops (small ivory levers raised or lowered by a finger) that control the various sounds which the organ can produce.

Johann Sebastian Bach 1685 - 1750

Born in Germany, into a large musical family, Johann Bach developed a love for music at an early age. He learned to play many different instruments when he was quite young. He also learned to sing. He was a very happy boy. He loved his big family gatherings which took place once a year. Just like we do on special holidays, all of his aunts and uncles and cousins would get together and eat fine meals, sing songs and play music.

After Bach's father died, he went to live with his brother who continued his musical training. Later, when he grew up, Johann married twice and had TWENTY-ONE children. Most of them were musicians, too.

Bach's Music

Much of Bach's music, written for voices and accompanied by the organ, was used in church services. It was Bach's job as a church organist to compose new sets of songs (called cantatas) regularly for the services of his church.

Bach also wrote many **fugues** and **toccatas**. A fugue is a kind of follow-the-leader piece. A melody is played and is followed by itself again and again. (It is similar to a "round" such as "Three Blind Mice", but more complicated. It is for the organ or other instruments, not usually for voices.) A toccata is a piece written for an instrument to let the performer "show off".

Bach composed many complicated cantatas, fugues, and toccatas, but he also wrote some simple tunes for his wife Anna to play. Piano students still enjoy playing these today.

Suggested Listening: Bach's *Toccata and Fugue in D minor* (You may find that it sounds like background music for a spooky ghost story.)

George Frederick Handel 1685 - 1759

Handel was born in Germany in the same year Bach was born. Unlike Bach, he did not have a large family of his own. However, he loved children, especially poor little orphans. He had lots of "pretend" nieces and nephews.

Handel's father was a doctor, and he wanted his son to become a lawyer, but this made Handel most unhappy because he always wanted to be a musician. With the help of his loving Aunt Anna, his dream came true. She secretly brought him a little **clavichord.** He learned to play it very well. Later he became a great organist and composer of wonderful music.

Handel traveled a long way and spent many years in London, England. There he made friends with kings and noblemen and became a famous musician, composing most of his operas. When he died he was buried in the famous church called Westminster Abbey in London, where many other important people are also buried.

Clavichord: An early stringed keyboard instrument which was rectangular in shape. It was the first keyboard instrument on which it was possible to play loud and soft by changing the pressure on the keys.

Handel's Music

Handel composed many different kinds of music. He wrote more than forty **operas** during the time he spent in England. He composed many **oratorios** also. The one most performed today is the *Messiah,* which gives us the famous "Hallelujah Chorus." Do you know that when people hear this stirring piece of music they still stand up, just as they did when it was first heard way back in 1741?

Beside his "singing" music, Handel also wrote wonderful music for orchestras. One of his great orchestral works, *The Royal Fireworks Music,* was composed to celebrate a peace treaty signed by England and France. It was first performed in Green Park in London in April, 1749, and a spectacular fireworks display was planned for the occasion.

Opera: A drama or play in which most talking by actors is replaced by singing. There are choruses, duets and long solos. The orchestra accompanies most of the singing.

Oratorio: A story is told by singing like an opera. The story most often has a theme from Scripture (the Bible or other religious text). Costumes and scenery are not usually used.

Suggested listening: *The Royal Fireworks Music,* Overture

Activities

BACH

Draw a picture which the *Toccata and Fugue in D minor* suggest to you. (Doesn't the music sound spooky in parts?)

Get music manuscript paper (with the lines of the music staff) or draw the five lines of the staff yourself. Then use different crayons or markers to draw an abstract line for each of the voices or parts of a fugue. This should make a very interesting design, and it should be fun to see the various designs that different people come up with.

HANDEL

Draw a picture of fireworks bursting in the sky as you listen to the *Royal Fireworks*. (Pastel or oil crayon on colored construction paper is especially good for this, but white paper and crayons are fine also.)

Legend has it that musicians played Handel's *Water Music* while floating down the Thames River on a barge. Whether this is fact or fiction, it could certainly make an interesting picture. Can you draw this and show the king's delight in being entertained in this way by the musicians?

Baroque Period

Match the words which go with the composers

Had many children

Traveled a lot   **Bach**

Wrote a spooky sounding piece

Toccata

Green Park

Fugue

Aunt Anna   **Handel**

Organ

Westminster Abbey

Clavichord

Summary

Write what you have learned about this period.

_____
_____
_____
_____
_____
_____
_____
_____
_____
_____

_____
_____
_____
_____
_____
_____
_____
_____

Write what you have learned about one of the composers of this period.

Classical Composers

the Classical Period

The Classical period followed the Baroque period. Unlike the fancy, splendid, ornate Baroque, the Classical period was a very neat, orderly time. Artists, and particularly musicians, followed strict rules. Their works were pure and uncomplicated in form. Dances at this time, such as the popular **minuet,** followed simple patterns and steps.

Two important new kinds of music began during this classical period. One was the **sonata.** A sonata is a piece of music written in three or four movements (sections) for one or two instruments. The other new form of music was the **symphony.** It is a large composition written in three or four movements for an orchestra. (a group of musicians playing different musical instruments.)

Two great musicians of the Classical era are Franz Joseph Haydn and Wolfgang Amadeus Mozart. Let's get to know these men and their music.

Suggested listening: Mozart's *Sonata in C*

the Classical Orchestra

The orchestra as we think of it today was established during the Classical Period, but it consisted of only about thirty or forty players. It was the most developed and composed-for "instrument" of that time. Haydn is credited with grouping the instruments of the orchestra into a pattern or form still used in our modern symphony orchestra. The classical orchestra was suited to the size of the salons (small parlors) of the titled and wealthy people for whom the music was performed. In Haydn's time large concert halls and auditoriums were practically non-existant. Later, as these were built, composers merely added more instruments to each group of the orchestra to increase its sound. The 20th century orchestra consists of 100 or more players. Imagine how Haydn would have felt hearing his music performed by such a large group of players!

The largest section of Haydn's classical orchestra was composed of the usual string choir, (violins, violas, cellos and bass), a woodwind section of six players (two flutes, two oboes, two bassoons), a brass section of four (two horns and two trumpets), and a percussion section consisting of a pair of kettle drums. Thus he used the orchestra as one great instrument, a perfect medium for a symphony.

Franz Joseph Haydn 1732 - 1809

Long, long ago, in a little town called Rohrau in Austria, a baby was born named Franz Joseph Haydn. His family was very poor, but in spite of this he was to become a great composer of beautiful music. He sang in a children's choir when he was only eight years old. Later he went to live in a beautiful palace owned by Prince Esterhazy. There he was paid to conduct an orchestra and to write as much music as he could. Wasn't he lucky?

Haydn lived at the palace for nearly thirty years, and didn't travel much, but when he was about sixty years old he accepted and invitation to go to London, England, to compose some symphonies and conduct some public concerts. It was very exciting for Haydn, as London was the largest city in 1791 and had fine orchestras. During that visit and a second one a few years later he wrote his famous "London" Symphonies.

Suggested listening: *Toy Symphony*, 1st Movement

Haydn's Music

Franz Joseph Haydn was the father of the symphony. He was nicknamed "Papa" Haydn. He composed many beautiful symphonies, over a hundred of them! No wonder he was called Papa Haydn! He also composed pieces for the **harpsichord** and many other kinds of music as well. His music followed the strict rules of his time. (Just as good sports have to follow the rules of the games they play, so also did Haydn have to follow the rules for writing certain kinds of music.)

harpsichord   A keyboard instrument which was popular during the 16th - 18th centuries, sometimes considered the "father" of the piano. However, the strings of the harpsichord are plucked by little quills, and the sound is not so loud as that of the piano.

Suggested listening: *Symphony No. 94 in G, "Surprise Symphony", 2nd movement*

Wolfgang Amadeus Mozart 1756 - 1791

In 1762, a concert for the great Elector was about to take place in Munich. Many people gathered to hear the performance. What do you think they thought when a little six year old boy scrambled up on a stool before a harpsichord, bowed his head to the audience, and began to play? Well, this little Austrian born boy was the child **prodigy** Mozart, who was to become one of the world's greatest performers and composers. However, as he outgrew being a cute little boy-genius, he was no longer in popular demand. He did not make much money and died a poor, poor man when he was only thirty-five years old. How sad to think that he was alone, and no one even knows where he was buried.

Prodigy: Unusual or extraordinary, a marvel. A child prodigy has unusual skill at something at a very young age.

Mozart's Music

Like Papa Haydn, Mozart composed some of the most beautiful sonatas and symphonies that we can hear today. He also wrote wonderful operas and **masses** for the church. One of his most popular operas is *The Magic Flute,* a fantasy filled with enchanting tunes. In the opera a magic flute helps a young prince get through some difficult experiences. Many people think this amusing opera is Mozart's best. Isn't it touching that he could write music for a funny opera at a time when he was not well and in debt? He wrote *The Magic Flute* the year he died.

Mozart's symphonies show how he followed the rules and plans of the time, like Papa Haydn. How neat and orderly his music sounds. The amazing thing is that Mozart could compose symphonies so quickly. Do you know that during six weeks (less time than the Fourth of July until the start of school) he completed three entire symphonies!

Mass: music for the parts of the Roman Catholic church service which has the sacrament of Holy Communion.

Suggested listening: *Symphony No. 40 in G minor,* 3rd Movement

Magic Flute, Papageno's Song

Activities

HAYDN

Supposedly the loud chords in the *Surprise Symphony* awakened drowsy, inattentive concert goers. Can you make three or four cartoon frames showing the sequence of events, 1) sleepy concert audience, 2) musicians playing loud chords, 3) surprised, awakened concert goers, 4) Haydn, pleased by his little surprise he gave everyone.

Listen to the *Toy Symphony,* and write down the names of the toys which come to mind for you as you listen. Can you tell why the music made you think of these toys?

MOZART

In *The Magic Flute* the bird catcher plays a magic flute to attract the birds. Can you draw the birds coming to him?

Think about what it must have been like for Mozart to be a child prodigy. He was dressed up in fancy clothes and gave concerts at fancy places when other children were doing very different things. Write a paragraph about how you think he must have felt. Do you think he liked being different or not?

Mozart wrote many other operas beside *The Magic Flute.* Find out what one of his other famous operas is, and learn the story of the opera.

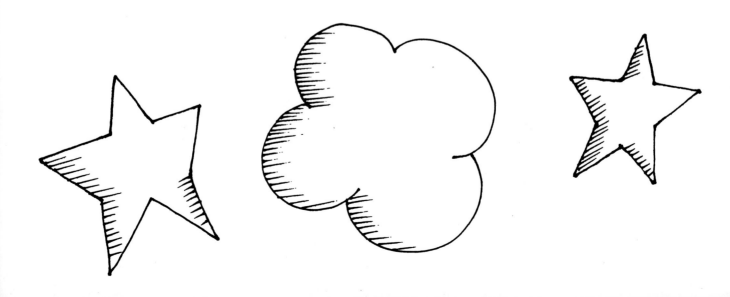

Classical Period

1. Two new forms of music began during the classical period. They were the _____ and the _____.

2. Haydn lived in Prince Esterhazy's beautiful _____.

3. The _____ was an important classical instrument.

4. Mozart was a child _____.

5. The classical period was very _____ and _____, following strict rules.

6. Mozart composed _____ for the Catholic Church service.

7. _____ composed the London Symphonies

8. _____ composed wonderful operas.

Where was the palace that Haydn lived in?

Answers: sonata, symphony; palace; harpsichord; prodigy; neat, orderly; masses; Haydn; Mozart

Summary

Write what you have learned about this period.

_____
_____
_____
_____
_____
_____
_____
_____
_____
_____
_____
_____
_____
_____
_____
_____
_____
_____

Write what you have learned about one of the composers of this period.

Romantic Composers

Beethoven
Schubert
Berlioz
Mendelssohn
Chopin
Schumann
Liszt
Brahms

and other people
of their time:

_____
_____
_____
_____

Name Some! There're lots!

the Romantic Period

The exciting, thrilling Romantic Period came after the strict, rule-abiding Classical Era. Instead of writing music which followed very definite patterns or forms, composers of the Romantic Period were more concerned with how the music made them feel inside. . . . It was very dramatic and spectacular. The orchestra used many more instruments to make bigger sounds. The music would be very loud and then very quiet. It would be very fast and then very slow. Operas became important, and they were very melodramatic. This means death and tragedy were often used as themes. Super heroes and heroines were the main characters. Composers told stories of the super-natural in their music, using dragons and goblins and gods and goddesses as their characters.

Can you guess what particular musical instrument became very popular during the Romantic Period? Here is a hint. It is one which we take for granted today and which we find in most homes. Give up? Well, it was the piano! Do you know that at first about the only people who owned pianos were the kings and queens and princes and princesses? Many composers began writing music for this great instrument.

Let's meet some of the important musical geniuses of the Romantic Era.

Suggested listening: *Sonata No. 27 in F minor, "Appassionata"* - Beethoven

the Piano

Romantic Composers loved the piano.

In the year 1709, an Italian named Christofori invented an instrument close to the modern piano. It was called a "pianoforte" because, unlike the harpsichord, it could produce both soft (piano) and loud (forte) tones. Since the piano strings were struck rather than plucked, (like the harpsichord) wonderful contrasts in sound could be achieved. The earlier pianos still had the soft, bell-like tinkle of the clavichord. It was not until many years later that the piano improved and became the first keyboard instrument to be able to sustain or hold tones by means of pedals. I am sure that many of you have played a piano or taken piano lessons and if you have you will remember that there are three pedals which "hold" the keys. On the left is the soft pedal, which softens all the tones. The loud pedal is on the right and it strengthens all the tones. The middle pedal holds the individual notes.

From the time of Beethoven into the Romantic period the piano became possibly the most important musical instrument of all times. Many **concertos** were written for the piano and orchestra. Two types of pianos are the upright and the Baby Grand.

Concerto: Composition written for solo instrument and orchestra

Suggested listening: *Concerto No. 5 in E flat, "Emporer Concerto"* - Beethoven

Ludwig Van Beethoven 1770 - 1827

Do any of you take piano lessons, or study a musical instrument? If so, have you ever been punished for not practicing enough? I'll bet that if you had been, you wouldn't like your music lessons very much. This is what happened to poor little Beethoven. Born in Bonn, Germany, he had a very mean, drunken father who wanted him to be a famous child prodigy like Mozart. Often his father would beat him to force him to practice.

When Beethoven was sixteen years old, he went to Vienna to play for Mozart who was most impressed with his musical ability. Later Papa Haydn gave him lessons. However, his real talent was composing music rather than performing it.

Beethoven began to go deaf when he was only about twenty-six years old. However, in spite of his growing deafness and the fact that he heard only in his mind, he composed some of the most beautiful music ever written. He had a very hard life and was so poor! Because of his deafness, he became very gruff and cross and didn't have many friends. Isn't it amazing that a person who had such an unhappy life could produce such wonderful music?

Beethoven's Music

Beethoven only wrote nine symphonies, but they are among the most beautiful ever composed. His *Ninth Symphony*, which he never heard, has a wonderful singing part for many voices. He also composed concertos for piano and for violin. Isn't it unbelievable that he produced some of his greatest music after he became deaf?

Much of Beethoven's early music follows the strict rules of the formal classical period. However, his later music expresses much more feeling and emotion. This passionate and moving music points the way towards the next period which we shall study. It is called the Romantic Era. Thus we call Beethoven a bridge or link between the Classical and Romantic Periods.

Beethoven's *Ninth Symphony* has a theme which has become very familiar. I'll bet you know this as "Joyful, Joyful We Adore Thee."

Suggested listening: *Symphony No. 9 in D minor*, last movement.

Franz Joseph Schubert 1797 - 1828

Schubert was born in Austria and had many brothers and sisters. His childhood was a happy one, although his later life was not. He did not want to be a teacher like his father. He only wanted to compose music. And compose he did! Writing songs was as natural for Schubert as breathing and talking. However, as famous as his music is today, he never made a fortune during his life.

He and a group of "artist" friends lived together, sharing what little money they had for food. They met in the evenings at various coffee houses and beer gardens to discuss music and art. Schubert frequently would hear a song in his mind and, not having a tablet with him, would write the music on a tablecloth. Can you imagine how many of his wonderful six hundred songs were lost when the tablecloths were washed?

Suggested listening: *Serenade, Ave Maria*

Schubert's Music

Schubert wrote symphonies — the most famous of which is *The Unfinished* (Symphony Number Eight in B Minor.) It is called unfinished because it has only two movements, instead of the usual three or four movements of the traditional symphonies.

However, Schubert is especially famous for his other pieces of music, his songs, piano music, and **chamber music.** Writing more than six hundred songs, he was truly the "song writer" of his day. One of his most famous songs is called "The Trout." It is a poem set to music. The poem tells the story of a little fish's brave fight to keep from being hooked by a very clever fisherman. In Schubert's chamber piece, *"The Trout,"* there are five instruments playing, and the violin "sings" the song about the trout.

Chamber music: Music written for a small group of instruments to be played in a small "music chamber" or music room.

Suggested listening: *Trout Quintet*, 4th movement

Hector Berlioz 1803 - 1869

Berlioz, the son of a very respected and conventional doctor, was born in a little town in France called La Cote-Sant-Andre. His father wanted him to become a doctor, and Berlioz really tried to study medicine, but after a short term at a medical school in Paris he became convinced that he wanted to be a musician. He was always a very "different" young man. He wore strange, far-out clothes. He would not control his feelings and temper, even in public. His music was too loud and dramatic. He kept his hair too long and messy. In short what word can you think of to describe the kind of man he was? Would "hippie" do?

He was a typical product of the emotional Romantic Era.

Berlioz' Music

Like the dramatic man that Berlioz was, his music also was very dramatic, sometimes loud, then very soft, fast and then quite slow. Much of his music told a story which was often printed in a program for the audience to read. We call this **program music.**

He added many instruments to the orchestra. He wanted to have huge orchestras to perform his music. He had instruments play together that had never been combined before. Sometimes he even put horns in bags to produce a special sound!

When he conducted the orchestra, he frequently would become so angry with the musicians if they made a mistake that he would have a temper tantrum right on stage in front of the audience.

Berlioz had a great love in his life. Her name was Harriet Smithson, and he used a theme throughout his *Symphonie Fantastic* to represent "his beloved." This theme, which is repeated throughout the symphony, is known as "l' Idee fixe" (fixed idea). In the second movement of the symphony, "At the Ball," the "Idee Fixe" is heard several times. Berlioz must have been successful with the idea expressed, for Harriet did eventually marry him.

Suggested listening: *Symphonie Fantastic,* 2nd movement

Felix Mendelssohn 1809 - 1847

Mendelssohn was born in Berlin, Germany, to a wealthy and educated family. Musicians and writers often came to visit in his home. His first name, Felix, actually means happy, and that is exactly what he was. Unlike the other composers we have met, Mendelssohn never had to worry about money. Also, his family encouraged him to study music. He was even responsible for bringing Bach's music before the public. He had a wonderful homelife and a happy marriage.

Mendelssohn's happiness poured forth in his joyful Christmas Carol *Hark the Herald Angels Sing*, and also in his many overtures.

Overture: Music usually written as an introduction, or sometimes as an independent piece

Suggested listening: *Fingal's Cave*, Overture
Capriccio Brilliant, Op. 22

Mendelssohn's Music

Not only did Mendelssohn compose wonderful symphonies, oratorios, overtures, and piano music, he was also a great conductor. Have you ever been to a concert and watched the conductor waving a little thin stick up and down at the members of the orchestra? This little stick is called a baton. Well, Mendelssohn was the first to use a light piece of whale bone covered in white leather as his baton. This baton is used to beat time and to keep the players together.

Mendelssohn, like other Romantic composers, wrote program music. One of his most popular examples of program music is his *Midsummer Night's Dream*. This is music for a delightful play by the famous playwright, William Shakespeare.

Suggested listening: *A Midsummer Night's Dream*, "Wedding March"

Frederic Chopin 1810 - 1849

When Frederic was a little nine year old boy in his hometown near Warsaw, Poland, he was already well-known as a fine pianist. Once he was asked to play in a public concert. The little fellow was dressed with great care by his mother, who was not able to go to the concert. When he came home she asked him what the people liked best, and instead of naming one of his piano pieces he shouted with glee, "Mother, everyone was looking at my very first collar!"

When Chopin was nineteen or twenty, he went to Vienna to make himself known as a musician. Later he went to Paris where he performed, composed and taught. He was a charming talented gentleman and mothers begged for him to teach their daughters to play the piano. However, no one wanted to insult him by handing him money. The young students would secretly put his fee under his beautiful white kid gloves which he left on the mantlepiece.

Later in his life he developed tuberculosis. Not much was known about treating that disease then, and Chopin died from it when still such a young man.

Suggested listening: *Polonaise Militaire*

Chopin's Music

Chopin composed music almost entirely for the piano. He liked shorter pieces rather than long symphonies with several movements. He combined folk rhythms of his native Poland (such as in his **Mazurkas** and **Polonaises**) with the more polished sophisticated music of Paris (such as in his **etudes, waltzes** and **preludes**). His style is easy to recognize—very romantic and elegant—and one must have a light touch on the keyboard and very nimble fingers to play his music.

The great composer and music critic, Robert Schumann, helped to make Chopin's music known throughout Europe. After hearing Chopin play his own *Variations on a Theme of Mozart's,* Schumann was do delighted with Chopin, both as a composer and a performer, that he wrote a review of the concert beginning with these words: "Hats off, Gentlemen – a genius."

One of Chopin's most popular pieces, one which is played most often, is the very lovely *Butterfly Etude.*

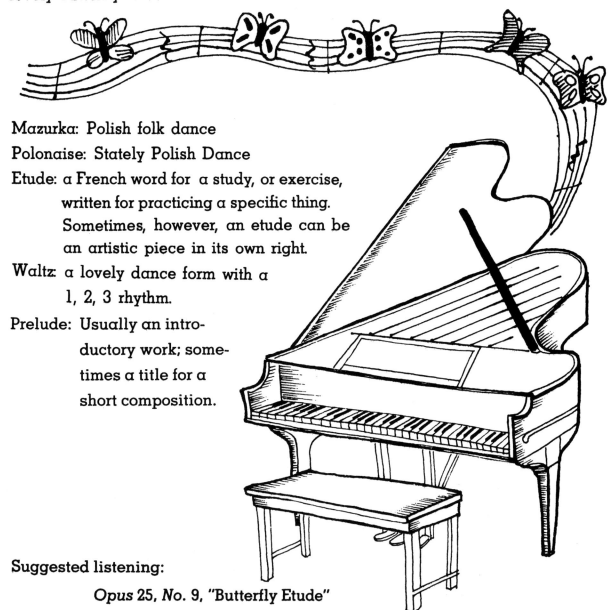

Mazurka: Polish folk dance

Polonaise: Stately Polish Dance

Etude: a French word for a study, or exercise, written for practicing a specific thing. Sometimes, however, an etude can be an artistic piece in its own right.

Waltz: a lovely dance form with a 1, 2, 3 rhythm.

Prelude: Usually an introductory work; sometimes a title for a short composition.

Suggested listening:

Opus 25, No. 9, "Butterfly Etude"

Robert Schumann 1810 - 1856

When Robert was a very young school boy in his hometown in Germany, he used to have fun playing "musical portraits" of his friends. How can someone "play" a "portrait"? Well if his friend was a mischievous, jovial sort of person, Robert wrote light, funny, happy-sounding music. If, however, his friend was very serious, he then wrote serious-sounding, slow music to "paint" his friend's musical portrait.

When he grew up, he fell in love and married Clara Wieck, the daughter of his piano teacher. Mr. Wieck opposed this marriage because Schumann was a penniless musician. Clara was a magnificient pianist, one of the first recognized female performers.

Poor Robert! He did not like being in second place to his wife. He wanted very much to be a concert pianist, but he damaged his fourth finger with a device designed to strengthen it. Therefore he had to give up playing and be a composer and music critic instead. He became so frustrated over this that he had to be placed in an insane asylum where he died. Isn't it unfortunate that someone who could write such beautiful, happy music as he did should have such an end to his life? Thank goodness Clara made his music popular by playing it in concerts all over Europe.

Schumann's Music

Schumann was one of the first composers who wrote piano music especially for children. He loved children, and his *Albumn for the Young, Carnaval,* and *Scenes from Childhood* have always been very popular with young people. He also composed symphonies and concertos which are filled with lovely melodies. Many **musicologists** (a long funny-sounding word which simply means someone who *writes* about music) have criticized Schumann's symphonies, saying he only wrote pretty melodies without much development of them. However, if you listen to his lovely *The Spring Symphony* (Symphony in B-flat Major, Op. 38) you will hear beautiful music filled with deep romantic feelings, and all the wonderful excitement that this happy season inspires in every one. Schumann, different from Beethoven, had his own personal style which was building up the orchestral music, brick by brick, with one enchanting melody after another.

Suggested listening: *Scenes From Childhood*, "Traumerei" (Reverie), "Hascheman" (Playing Tag)

Franz Liszt 1811 - 1886

By the time he was a young man in his early twenties, Franz Liszt, born in Hungary, was considered to be one of the greatest pianists of all time. When he came on stage, women screamed and swooned over him, much the same way teenagers have done in recent times over the Beatles or other pop and rock singers. They fought for some souvenir of his: a piece of his handkerchief – a glove – anything – and how he loved all this flattery!

Sometimes when Liszt would play a piano concert in a concert hall he would have two pianos, placed back to back on stage, so that he could play first on one, then on the other. By his doing this, everyone had a chance to watch his hands perform. He was truly a great artist!

Suggested listening: *Les Preludes*
Liebestraume

Liszt's Music

Liszt wrote some music for large orchestras, but mostly he composed for the piano. He was a musical genius both as a performer and as a composer. Some of his music was based on folk songs of his native Hungary. He took native folk songs and made them more elaborate, calling them rhapsodies. He also arranged great symphonic music and opera music for the piano.

We can all thank Liszt for a great contribution to the performing artist. He was the first pianist to turn the piano sideways so that the musician's back was no longer towards the audience. Wouldn't it be terrible if all we could see of a pianist were his back?

Suggested listening: *Hungarian Rhapsodies*

Johannes Brahms 1833 - 1897

Do you remember a family we met earlier – Clara and Robert Schumann? Well, these musical people became the most intimate of friends with Johannes Brahms, the German-born composer and pianist. Brahms met the Schumanns while he was on a concert tour, and he spent much time in their home. Brahms never married, and the Schumann children became his "pretend" nieces and nephews, sort of like Handel's relationship with many of his friends' children. After Robert Schumann was put into an insane asylum, Brahms, although he was much younger, tried to help Clara with her children. He also helped to popularize Schumann's music.

Brahms was fortunate to have had musical parents who encouraged him to be a musician, quite unlike the families of Handel or Berlioz. Other than music, Brahms enjoyed sports of all kinds, especially mountain climbing and swimming, and how he loved to joke and play tricks on his friends!!

It is sad to think that when he went to his dear friend Clara's funeral, he caught a cold, became quite ill from it and died as a result, prematurely. Nonetheless, he is remembered fondly as the third of the three B's of music. Can you name the other two?

Suggested listening: *Academic Festival Overture*

Brahms' Music

Brahms composed both orchestral music and songs. He also composed many piano **concertos.** His symphonies are frequently performed in concerts today and show much influence of Beethoven. Brahms preferred Beethoven's traditional type symphony to the program type symphony of Berlioz. He felt that music should not have to tell a story.

His *Academic Festival Overture* was written as a "thank you" to the University of Breslau in Germany for honoring him with a degree. He used college songs popular throughout Germany as his themes. One of his very popular and lovely songs is known as "Brahms' Lullaby." Most of you are probably familiar with it.

Concerto: Musical composition for orchestra and a solo instrument

Suggested listening: "Brahms' Lullaby"

Activities

BEETHOVEN

- Write a few sentences about how you think Beethoven must have felt about being deaf. Do you think he was brave to keep on writing music?

- Listen to the 1st movement of Beethoven's *Fifth Symphony*. Do you recognize this music? Have you heard it in any commercials or movies that you know?

SCHUBERT

- Listen to the 1st movement, *Trout Quintet*, and draw your own version of the fish.

- Schubert used to write out his ideas for new songs on the restaurant tablecloths if he had nothing else to write on. Can you write out a dialogue between Schubert and his waiter, or between the waiter and the restaurant manager, or the waiter and the washwoman when this happened?

BERLIOZ

- The *Symphonie Fantastique* has exotic, fantastic sounds. Can you draw a picture with fantastic shapes and color which the music suggests to you? This might be a good time to use water colors. Let the wet colors flow into one another.

MENDELSSOHN

- Pretend you are a musician writing to another musician and telling him about Mendelssohn's use of the baton. Tell if you liked it or not and why.

- *The Overture to a Midsummer Night's Dream* is about elves and fairies and their adventures. Can you draw a picture of what the music suggests to you?

CHOPIN

- Draw a butterfly joyfully moving about as suggested by Chopin's *Butterfly Etude*.
- Much of Chopin's music was inspired by the folk dances of his native Poland. Look up Folk Dancing in the encyclopedia and find out about folk dances of countries other than Poland. Why would folk dances inspire a composer?

SCHUMANN

- Schumann included in *Scenes from Childhood* games he remembered from his childhood such as Blind Man's Buff. What games from childhood would you include if you were to compose a piece of music by that title?

LISZT

- Pretend you are a newspaper reporter writing about the ladies swooning over Lizst's performances at a concert. Describe what took place.

- Sometimes when Lizst toured there would be a piano waiting at the train station, so that he could perform for people even at "whistle stops," – draw this scene.

BRAHMS

- Can you define a lullaby? Tell three characteristics you think a lullaby should have. Tell why.

- Draw a picture of another favorite lullaby such as "Go Tell Aunt Nancy" or "Rock a Bye Baby."

Romantic Period

Put an R before words which have to do with the Romantic Period

Put a C before words which have to do with the Classical Period

orderly	emotional
rules	piano
symphony	Berlioz
Haydn	baton
Mozart	pretend nieces & nephews
Harpsichord	Schumann

Summary

Write what you have learned about this period.

Write what you have learned about one of the composers of this period.

Nationalistic Composers

Verdi
Wagner
Strauss
Tchaikovsky
Rimsky-Korsakov
Grieg
Sibelius
Sullivan
Elgar

and other people
of their time:

Who else was famous then?

_____
_____
_____
_____

Nationalism

About the time that the Romantic Era was reaching its peak, a new period in world history, as well as music history, was developing. We call this new period the Nationalistic Era. Do any of you have any ideas about what this term means? Think of the word nation or national and what it implies. Basically, nationalism means patriotism or love of one's country. It meant, and means, expressing pride in one's own language, customs, literature, art and music. During the nineteenth century, authors wrote books using native folk legends and historical events and heroes of their own countries for subject matter. Classical literature, which had always been printed in its original language, was now translated into all languages of all nations. Artists painted pictures of things in their native land. In music, composers used native folk songs and folk dance forms for the basis of their great musical compositions. They looked for ways to express the feelings of their people in music.

As the map making industry improved, the boundaries of countries became more definite, and people living within these boundaries developed a fierce national pride in their country and its culture.

We shall meet some of these great nationalistic composers and listen to some of their music which helps to express the feelings and sentiments of the people in their own countries.

the Accordion

The accordion, a reed-type musical instrument, is worn on straps around the shoulders. It is seldom used in a symphony orchestra but is frequently played at parties as it is portable (able to be carried). Many musicians through Europe used it as an accompaniment for folk dancing and folk singing. It was this **folk music,** of the people, which inspired many of the nationalist composers we will study in this section.

The main parts of the accordion are the bellows, a piano keyboard, and a board of buttons. The bellows, located between the keyboard and buttons, pump air through the reeds. The piano-like keyboard, on one end, supplies the melody notes, while the buttons, on the other end, form the bass notes and chords. The sound is produced by opening and closing the bellows. There are two sets of reeds in the bellows, one that plays when it is being opened and one which plays when it is being closed. The vibrations of these metal reeds produce sounds.

Guiseppi Verdi 1813 - 1901

Did any of you ever, when you were younger, try to do something which you could not do and have it make you so angry that you wanted to hit something? Well, believe it or not, this same thing happened to Verdi when he was a very young boy. In the little Italian village, Roncole, where Verdi was born, his parents ran a small inn and sold groceries. Their son showed a great talent for music, so they sacrificed things for themselves in order to buy Guiseppi an old **spinet** (a sort of harpsichord). One day, when he was putting some notes together to form chords, he found one he liked very much. However, when he tried to find this chord again, he could not do so, and he flew into a childish rage. In frustration he grabbed a hammer and began to smash the spinet. His father came into the room just in time and stopped him before he had damaged it too badly. After that he took good care of his musical instrument, and when he died many years later, it was still in his possession.

Fortunately for music lovers the world over, Verdi outgrew these childish tantrums and went on to produce some of the greatest operas ever written.

Suggested listening: *La Traviata* – Act I, Scene I

Verdi's Music

Italy was divided into many little states, and some of them were under Austrian rule. Verdi, through his music, worked towards freeing Italy.

He wrote altogether thirty operas, and most of them cleverly concealed hidden patriotic meanings. *Nabucco* told the story of the ancient Jews in captivity but really implied the captivity of the Italians by the Austrians. *Rigoletto* was objected to by the Austrian authorities because the king in the opera was pictured to be a villain. And of course Verdi was certain to be a popular liberation hero when the letters of his last name became a national slogan. VITTORIO EMMANUEL RE D'ITALIA— Victor Emmanuel, King of Italy. In fact, he was such a popular hero that his death in Milan, Italy, was the occasion for national mourning.

Other beloved operas include *La Traviata, Il Trovatore, Othello* and *Aida*

Suggested listening: *Aida,* "Grand March"

Richard Wagner 1813 - 1883

Superman! Superhero! Super music! Super big orchestra! Super long story! All of these "supers" tell us about the German born Richard Wagner, the man and the musician. One of the great Nationalistic Composers, Wagner wrote fantastic operas which he called music dramas! He thought that the German people were the super race – the strongest, the smartest, and the bravest! and he based his music dramas on these characteristics.

When Wagner was a young teenager he wrote his first play, a tragedy with forty-two characters. He was always thinking about play-writing, and he had much encouragement from his step-father who was an actor. Later, he heard Beethoven's music which was full of feeling and it influenced Wagner. He met Franz Liszt (remember him?) who performed his music, and people realized how beautiful it was. Being a gambler Wagner was often out of money. However, he did have some good luck. King Ludwig II of Bavaria recognized his genius and offered him a theater, a salary to write music, and the freedom to produce his music dramas. Doesn't that sound like a fairy tale? Imagine having a king want to do such wonderful things for a musician!

In 1870 Wagner married a lady named Cosima, who was the daughter of Liszt, and together they lived in the small Bavarian town of Bayreuth. Here the famous Wagnerian opera festivals are held. In 1882 Wagner's poor health caused him to travel to sunny Italy in hopes of getting well. However, he died quite suddenly in Venice in February, 1883.

Suggested listening, *Meistersingers*, Overture

Wagner's Music

Crashing symbols! Whispering strings – Blaring tubas! Moaning oboes – Thundering drums! Great contrasts! These are the sounds of Wagner's huge, grand orchestra. Longer pieces of music, more complicated stories (based on German legends and folklore), elegantly styled costumes, elaborate scenery, all these arts should be equally important in his music dramas – this was Wagner's feelings. He wrote his own **librettos** in German, designed his own sets, and conducted his own orchestra, as well as composing his own music.

Another contribution, a musical expression called a **leitmotif**, was made by Wagner. The leitmotif is a German word meaning a short musical theme which represents a certain character, place, idea, or object. These themes recur (occur again and again) throughout Wagner's music dramas and help us understand the complicated stories.

One of the famous operas written by Wagner is *Lohengrin*. In Lohengrin the maiden Elsa is wrongly accused of murdering her brother, but at her trial the hero Lohengrin arrives to defend her. You recognize the melody as "Here Comes the Bride."

libretto: written text of an opera

Suggested listening: *Lohengrin*, Prelude

Johann Strauss, Jr. 1825 - 1899

Born in Vienna, Johann became the most famous musician of a famous musical family. His father, Johann the elder, composed waltzes and organized a band to conduct them. He tried to discourage young Johann from following a career in music, but he would not listen to his father. He learned to play the violin and studied the art of composing music. By the time he was only nineteen, (when most young men of today are entering their second year of college) he had a job playing the violin in a restaurant and conducting his own group of musicians. When his father died in 1849, the then twenty-four year old Johann combined his band with his father's. He composed delightful dance music which helped its listeners to feel the beauty of his beloved Vienna. He became known as the "Waltz King."

Suggested listening: *The Blue Danube*

Strauss' Music

Imagine, if you will, a large ball room with sparkling crystal chandeliers casting picturesque shadows on the walls. The room is filled with Viennese ladies in beautiful ball gowns and Viennese gentlemen in their handsome formal attire, waiting for the orchestra to begin. The conductor, Johann, Jr. appears, makes a small bow to the assembled guests, turns towards his musicians, lifts his baton, and suddenly the lilting refrain of his glorious waltz, *Tales of the Vienna Woods*, begins. Instantly, the room is in motion as the couples sway to and fro, waltzing to the delightful strains of his joyous music. This was the Vienna of Johann Strauss — happy, beautiful, care-free, uncomplicated by politics and war. Is it any wonder that he was known as the Waltz King?

In all, he composed nearly 500 works of music, including waltzes, polkas, and operettas. His light, uplifting music helps us to know a very different outlook on life from the more somber one of Richard Wagner.

Suggested listening: *Tales of the Vienna Woods*

Peter Ilyitch Tchaikovsky 1840 - 1893

Has anyone of you ever had a pen pal? Do any of you know what a pen pal is? A pen pal is a friend you make through writing letters — someone you have not met and someone whom you may never meet. Thanks to a wonderful pen pal, Madame Nadejda Von Meck, Tchaikovsky, the Russian-born composer, was provided with a large sum of money which enabled him to concentrate on composing his great, emotional, orchestral music. Mme. Von Meck was Moscow's foremost music lover, and, after hearing Tchaikovsky's beautiful, often sad Russian music, she insisted upon helping him. However, she also insisted that they never meet. This arrangement suited him as he was always very shy with people.

His family did not want him to be a musician. However, after his mother's death, which caused him great sadness, he rebelled and studied music quite seriously. He was a very unhappy man and could not keep many friends. When his friendship with Mme. Von Meck ended, he decided to come to America in 1891 to escape his deep despair. It was during this visit that he conducted his own *1812 Overture* at the opening of our great Carnegie Hall in New York. Eventually he returned to Russia and died in 1893.

Tchaikovsky is probably best remembered for his delightful, happy *Nutcracker Suite* (or **Ballet**). How amazing that someone who's life was filled with such sadness could leave to the world music that was filled with such joy.

Ballet: A story danced to music

Suggested listening: Selections from the *Nutcracker Ballet*, "Overture", "Dance of the Sugar Plum Fairies"

Tchaikovsky's Music

Tchaikovsky's beautiful music was very nationalistic and Russian in feeling. Much of it was sad and gloomy. He composed six great symphonies, one of which he called the *Pathetique*. In the first movement he introduced a small part of a Russian funeral service. In his very popular ballet, *The Nutcracker*, (have any of you ever seen or heard this especially at Christmas time?) there is one section, an electrifying Russian dance, called the "Trepak." The finale of his *Concerto No. 1 for Piano and Orchestra* begins with a Russian folk-type dance. His thrilling *1812 Overture*, written to celebrate Russia's victory over Napoleon, is filled with the clanging of the Moscow church bells and patriotic strains of the Russian National Anthem.

Tchaikovsky even planned for cannons to boom in accompaniment when the Overture was performed outdoors.

Suggested listening: *1812 Overture*

Nicholas Rimsky-Korsakov 1844 - 1908

Can you guess what Rimsky-Korsakov's profession was when he became the first Russian composer to write a symphony? I'll bet many of you thought he was a music professor or conductor, or possibly had a patron (like Papa Haydn had) who paid him to compose. Well, guess again! He was an attractive young Russian naval officer and was on a voyage at sea when he wrote his first symphony. Even though he composed a considerable amount of music while he was connected with the Russian Naval Forces, he wanted to retire so that he could concentrate on a life of music. Two years before he left the navy he was appointed professor of composition and orchestration at the St. Petersburg Conservatory. He also belonged to a group of Russian Nationalist Composers known as "The Russian Five."

Rimsky-Korsakov was fortunate in that he was born into a cultured and aristocratic family and was given piano lessons when quite young. He was exposed to all of the arts. His early musical training, both in piano and conducting, helped him later in his navy career, as he was put in charge of directing the marine bands. He even went to the Paris World's Fair in 1889 and conducted a Russian orchestra in a program of nationalistic music.

Suggested listening: *Tsar Sultan,* "Flight of the Bumble Bee"

Rimsky-Korsakov's Music

Very nationalistic in flavor, most of Rimsky-Korsakov's music is based on Russian folk tunes. He composed symphonies, operas, and symphonic poems, the most popular of which is *Scheherazade*. It is a **symphonic poem** picturing four stories from **The Arabian Nights**. Have any of you ever read **The Arabian Nights**? The tales of Alladin and Sinbad the Sailor are stories in this collection.

Scheherazade was a princess doomed by her husband, the Sultan, to die after her wedding night, but she cleverly postponed her fate by telling him "cliff-hanger" tales. Each night she ended her tales at the most exciting moment, and her husband decided not to have her executed until he heard the end of the story. The following evening she completed one story, but began another. (Eventually the sultan decided not to kill her.)

Symphonic or tone poem: A piece of program music for orchestra, written in one movement, suggesting a scene or creating a mood.

Suggested listening: *Scheherazade*, 1st Movement

Edward Grieg 1843 - 1907

When Grieg, born in Bergen, Norway, was only a little five year old boy, he began to show a deep interest in music while listening to his talented mother play the piano. He put notes together to make lovely chords. Later, when he began to take piano lessons from his mother, he found that he didn't like to practice day after day. He wanted to make up little tunes instead. However, his mother insisted that he practice exercises and scales, and thank goodness she did! Otherwise he might never have learned enough to compose the beautiful music which we have today.

Grieg was sent to study at the Leipzig Conservatory in Germany. Later, after an unsuccessful concert in Bergen, he went to Copenhagen, Denmark. While there he really developed a deep interest in his native Norwegian folklore, song and culture. He then began to make use of these elements in his music.

He married his cousin Nina, a singer, and they returned to Norway. He became a prosperous and famous musician. Unlike so many composers we have studied, Grieg's life was happy, successful and full of the joy of living and loving.

Suggested listening: *Piano Concerto A minor* – 1st movement

Grieg's Music

Grieg was a very patrotic Norwegian. Even though most of his musical training was done in Germany and Denmark, he wrote real Norwegian music. He loved the folk songs of his native land and often went into the country to hear the peasants sing them. *Two Norwegian Melodies*, for solo strings and orchestral accompaniment are built on actual folk songs. His great masterpiece, the *Piano Concerto in A minor*, makes use of two folk-like tunes in the last movement. Another piece, *The Song of Norway*, truly tells of Grieg's deep love for his country.

Grieg also wrote **incidental music** for the Norwegian classic *Peer Gynt*, by Norway's most famous author, Henrik Ibsen. The story is based on a Norwegian lengendary character, Peer Gynt, who is a boy quite difficult for his mother to handle. He lies and gets in lots of trouble.

incidental music: Music written as a background for a play or movie to set a mood

Suggested listening: Selections from *Peer Gynt Suite*

Jean Sibelius 1865 - 1957

Finland, the birthplace of Jean Sibelius, is a small country lying way to the north of Europe. Finland shares a border with Russia, the country which dominated it and forced cruel rules upon its people. The struggle of Finland to free itself from Russian rule was the drive which led Sibelius to become a musical nationalist.

He became such an outstanding composer that the Finnish government gave him a life-time pension so that he could devote himself completely to composition. He married the daughter of a Finnish composer, and together they built a home in the Finnish forest which Sibelius loved so dearly. After a concert tour of Europe and America he returned to his home, Villa Ainola, living happily and peacefully until his death at age ninety-one.

Sibelius' Music

Sibelius has been regarded as a National hero of Finland, having parks, streets, and museums named for him. Do you know that a postage stamp bearing his likeness was made during his lifetime? This is because he composed so much music which was based on Finnish legends, and because his famous *Finlandia Op. 26* represents Finland to the world. It expressed the hope for freedom and liberty stirring in all Finnish hearts.

He composed symphonies which have brooding themes suggesting the quiet peaceful forest of the countrysides of Finland.

Suggested listening: *Finlandia*

Sir Arthur Sullivan 1842 - 1900

It might be fun to write music one day.

Born in London, young Arthur Sullivan was fortunate in having a father who was the bandmaster for the Royal Military College of Sandhurst, near London – (our West Point equivalent). He loved to spend hours listening to the band practice and as a result learned to play many instruments. His knowledge of British Military music and orchestration grew. We can hear his love of instruments in his later comic operas.

He won a Mendelssohn (remember him?) scholarship to study at the famous Leipzig Conservatory in Germany and was a classmate of Edward Grieg (remember him, too?). There he learned to write effectively for the chorus. This choral writing and his clever orchestrations have become trademarks of the beloved Gilbert And Sullivan **Operettas.** (See next page.)

His works became so popular throughout England that Queen Victoria made him a knight.

Gilbert and Sullivan's Music

Have you ever been to an operetta? Do you know what an **operetta** is? It is a light, usually humorous play set to music. It is different from opera. It has a lot of "talking" (spoken dialogue). The music is usually appealing and "singable." The plot is amusing and romantic. One of the earlier operettas, *Die Fledermaus* (The Bat), was written by "The Waltz King." Do you remember who he was? However, the most popular operettas for audiences the world over were written by the English composer Arthur Sullivan, and W. S. Gilbert, the librettist, the man who wrote the words. Together they became known as Gilbert and Sullivan. Most of their operettas dealt with poking fun at English politics and traditions. *Trial by Jury* was concerned with the English courts. *H.M.S. Pinafore* joked about the Royal Navy. *The Gondoliers* made fun of Royalty, and *The Mikado* laughed at British society in Japanese disguise.

When you listen to selections from these operettas, try to follow the words of the songs. Can you imagine how difficult it would be to sing such long lines of music without running out of breath?

Suggested listening: H.M.S. Pinafore, "Captain of the Pinafore"

Sir Edward Elgar 1857 - 1934

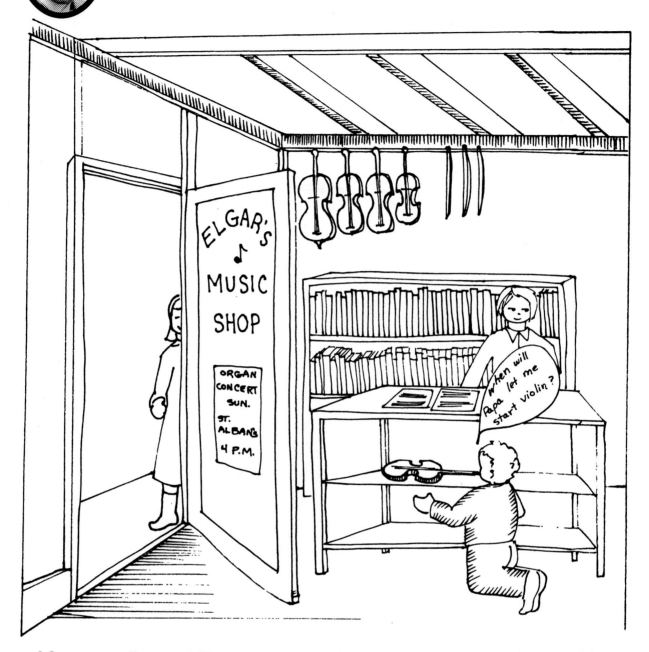

Music was all around Elgar. Born in Broadheath, the son of an organist and music seller, he heard music constantly talked about in his father's shop. As a little boy he listened to his father play the organ. Nearly all the family conversation at mealtimes centered on music. He himself studied the violin and the piano, and became known as a fine accompanist. Is it any wonder, then, that he gave up the study of law in favor of a career in music? He settled down to the business of seriously composing orchestral works. Through his compositions and study of music Elgar helped make England a cultural center for music.

Suggested listening: *The Enigma Variations*

Elgar's Music

Elgar shows nationalistic traits in his music by using subjects related to English national legend or art. These are seen in his choral works, *The Banner of St. George*, and his symphonic poem, *Falstaff.* A concert overture, *Cockaigne,* is nationalistic in that it is a musical description of London. In addition to these, he composed many orchestral works displaying such typical English traits as a keen sense of humor and a certain kind of vigor. This is especially noted in his world-famous symphonic march, *Pomp and Circumstance.* The main melody is played most often for graduation.

Suggested listening: *Pomp and Circumstance*, March No. 1

Activities

VERDI

Verdi was an Italian patriot with a great love for his country. This love of his country was evident in his music. Can you name some American songs which also show patriotism?

WAGNER

In *Lohengrin* the swan is really Elsa's bewitched brother. Write a paragraph about what the brother must think of being turned into a swan.

STRAUSS

Draw a scene suggesting River Danube, which is depicted in *The Blue Danube*.

TCHAIKOWSKY

Find out the names of some of the dances in *The Nutcracker.*

Find out what happened in 1812 in Russia which caused Tchaikowsky to write his joyful *1812 Overture.*

RIMSKY-KORSAKOV

Read some stories from *The Arabian Nights,* especially "Sinbad."

Make up your own version of a marvelous escape which Sinbad experienced.

GRIEG

Draw a rugged mountain scene which might be similar to the mountains Peer Gynt explored.

Peer Gynt meets some wretched trolls when he is in the mountains. Can you draw your version of a troll?

SIBELIUS

Sibelius chose to live most of his life in his villa in a peaceful forest? Why do you suppose a composer would choose this setting for his home instead of a bustling city?

Suppose you were the artist chosen to design the postage stamp in Sibelius' honor. What would you draw? Can you make a sample stamp?

SULLIVAN

Sullivan wrote operettas rather than operas. Explain the difference between the two.

Find out the story of *H.M.S. Pinafore.* Why is Buttercup an important character in the story?

ELGAR

Elgar is famous for *Pomp and Circumstances,* and this piece of music is played at graduations. Listen to the music and tell why you think it is appropriate for such occasions. Is it dignified? Is it happy? What words can you think of to describe this music?

Nationalistic Period

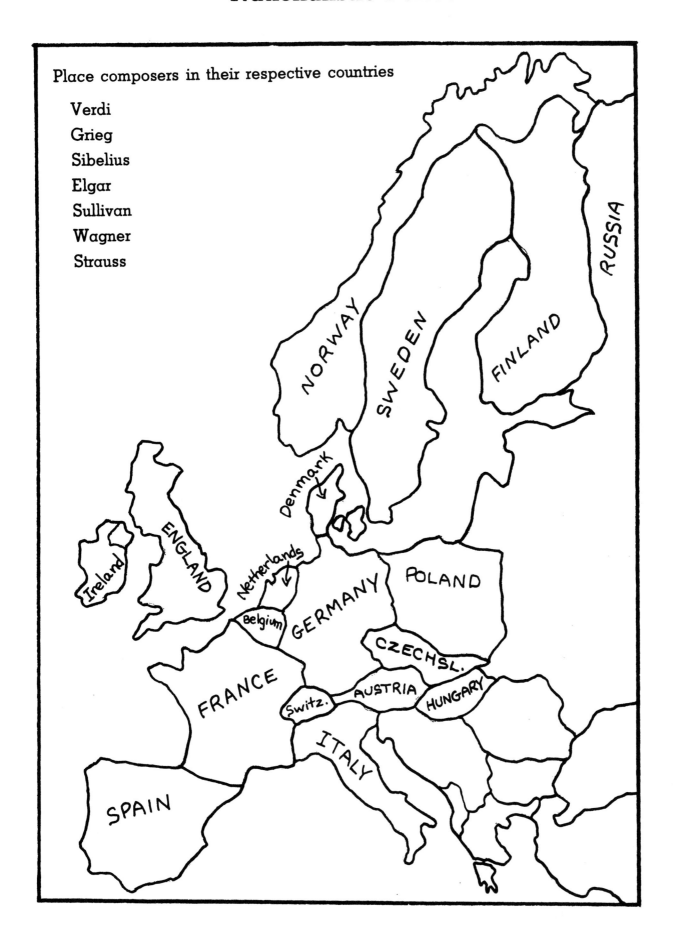

Place composers in their respective countries

- Verdi
- Grieg
- Sibelius
- Elgar
- Sullivan
- Wagner
- Strauss

Summary

Write what you have learned about this period.

Write what you have learned about one of the composers of this period.

Impressionist Composers

Debussy
Ravel

and other people of their time:

_____

_____

_____

_____

_____

Who else made the headlines?

Impressionism

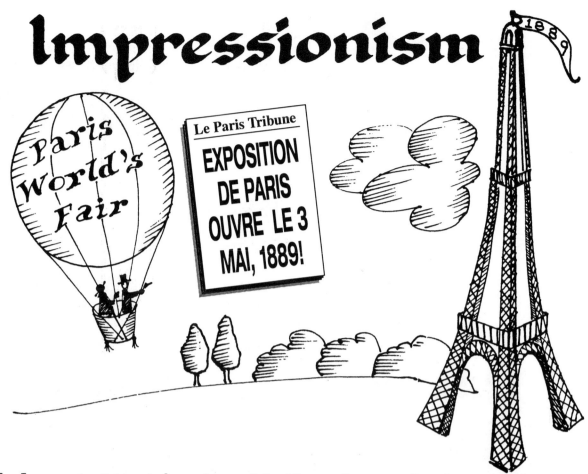

The Impressionist period overlapped the Nationalist period and continued on into the twentieth century. It was a time when art and music created hazy impressions and moods.

Do any of you know what an impression is? It is an idea or feeling without any definite shape or form – fleeting glimpses – misty shadows – foggy landscapes – suggestions rather than lines. These are some of many phrases used to describe the art of the Impressionistic Period in the late nineteenth and early twentieth centuries, the art of painters such a Manet, Monet and Renoir. The music of this era was affected by the great impressionist painters and their lack of concern for form and tradition. Dreamy melodies – delicate strings – misty harmonies – gentle sounds – flutes and oboes, rather than blaring trumpets or roaring drums, these are some of the phrases which describe this impressionist music.

Claude Debussy is the composer who is credited with originating impressionism in music. Maurice Ravel continued this style. Let us meet these two remarkable French composers and learn something about them and their music.

When the Paris World's Fair opened in 1889, Debussy was tremendously excited by the music he heard played by foreigners at the fair. It was the players from Java who really interested him most with their **gamelan** orchestra. They too helped pave the way for Impressionism.

gamelan: a xylophone type instrument played in Java (one of the Indonesian Islands in the South Pacific.)

the Harp

Have you ever seen pictures of angels sitting before a harp with their fingers on the strings? And if so, have you ever wondered why a harp rather than a tuba or a bassoon or even a violin was pictured with angels? Well, to understand why you must either listen to the heavenly sound that can be made on a harp or know something about the sound and the instrument.

Harps have their origins or beginnings in very ancient times. There are even many references to the harp in the Bible. The earliest Egyptian ones ranged in size from smaller shoulder harps of seven strings to very fancy standing instruments with twenty-two strings.

The harp, as we know it, is a very tall, triangular-shaped instrument with forty-six strings. These strings make that lovely, heavenly sound when plucked with the fingers of both hands. There are seven pedals at the base which change the pitch (the highness or lowness) of the strings. The beautiful, misty, impressionistic music of Debussy makes good use of this wonderful, stringed musical instrument.

Claude Achille Debussy 1862 - 1918

When he was a little boy, Debussy, who was born to poor parents in a suburb of Paris, showed great musical talent. His father even thought that if his son were a performing prodigy he could make a hugh fortune off of his talent. However, Mr. Debussy was in for a disappointment because young Claude never became a concert pianist. His gift lay in his musical imagination and composition rather than in his ability as a performer. Thank goodness an aunt recognized his talent and sent him to the Paris conservatory to study. He was a brilliant student, determined to compose music from his own ideas rather than following the school's rules. He was rewarded in 1884 by winning the very sought after **"Prix de Rome."** This was a prize awarded by the French government to a music student to study in Rome. However, Debussy did not like Rome and left before his time of study was completed. He returned to his beloved Paris and became a familiar figure in all of his favorite cafes.

Although he was a quiet, mild mannered person, he was known as a "character." He dressed like a "Bohemian," displayed a passion for cats and smoked constantly. He married twice and had one daughter but, sadly, developed cancer, which caused him much pain and suffering in the last years of his life.

Suggested listening: *Clair de Lune*

Debussy's Music

Debussy, from the time he was a young boy wanted to write a totally new kind of music—free from strict forms, free from the excess of German romantic emotionalism—to be rid of the booming sounds of Wagner. His music has often been described as vague, hazy and misty. He shows the influence of the impressionist painters Monet, Manet and Renoir, who loved to paint scenes of nature and of everyday life. Debussy also chose to picture nature in his music, especially the sounds of wind and waves in *La Mer* (The Sea), the mists and clouds in *Three Nocturnes*, and the light of the moon in *Clair de Lune*.

One of his most expressive works is the beautiful, the delicate *L'Apres Midi d'un Faune* (The Afternoon of a Fawn). It describes the feelings of a young deer lazily stretching and day-dreaming on a hot, muggy summer day.

Suggested listening: *Afternoon of a Fawn*

Maurice Ravel 1875 - 1937

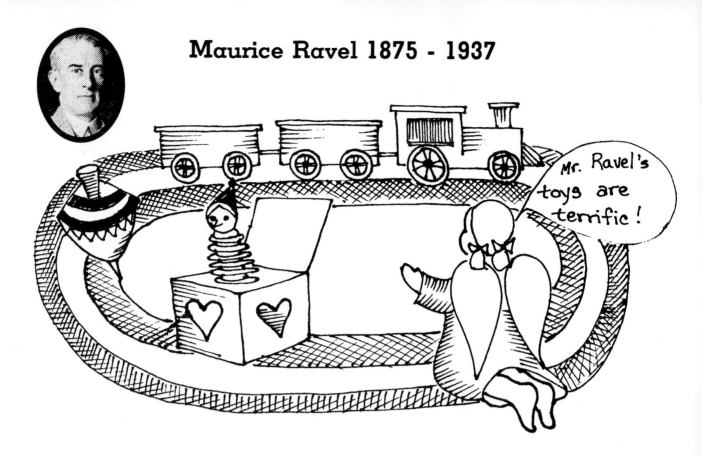

How many of you have tried over and over to make the honor role or a sports team or to win a prize, only to fail in each repeated effort? If anything like this has happened to you then you can understand the disappointment Maurice Ravel, the great impressionist composer, must have suffered. He tried four separate times to win the Prix de Rome (remember that?) but failed each and every time. Imagine how discouraging these failures must have been for him! Fortunately for the music world, he shrugged off his failures and went on with his work.

Born in France, near the border of Spain, Ravel was a follower of Debussy. He was a very small man, only five feet tall. Probably because of being so short he was very particular about his appearance. He would spend hours selecting properly matched clothes and making sure that they fit him just right. He was just as particular about neatness and cleanliness in his own home. He was probably equally as choosy about a wife, for he never married.

During World War I, Ravel was a member of the motor corps and served at the battlefront. He never forgot the gruesome sights he saw, and they caused him some depression and sadness all of his life.

However, one of the brightest parts of his life was his love of children, just as it was with Handel and Brahms. He also loved children's toys and had quite a large collection of electric trains and other treasures which brought squeals of delight to youngsters of all ages who were lucky enough to know Ravel and visit him.

Suggested listening: *Ma Mere L'Oye,* (Mother Goose Suite)

Ravel's Music

Ravel was considered to be an Impressionist composer because of his harmony and orchestration which were similar to Debussy's. He was also able to create impressions and moods while following some older musical forms. His lovely, dreamy *La Valse (The Waltz)* shows his impressionistic style and was written as a tribute to the great Waltz King. (Do you remember who he was?) His affection for children is shown in his lovable orchestral work *Ma Mere L'Oye (Mother Goose)*.

Having been born near Spain, his music definitely shows that country's influence, especially in his opera *L'Heure Espagnole (Spanish Hour)* and his orchestral work *Bolero. Bolero*, originally written for a famous dancer, is based on two Spanish style melodies. They are played in a definite Spanish rhythm repeated over and over. The melodies, first heard by the flute and clarinet, pass from one group of instruments to another. Gradually more and more instruments are added each time the melodies are played. Ravel was not really pleased with Bolero. Even though it was commissioned as a ballet he wrote it almost as an exercise and was sad that people remembered him chiefly for that piece of music.

Suggested listening: *Bolero*

Suggested Activities

DEBUSSY

Can you draw a peaceful forest scene which *Afternoon of a Fawn* suggests?

Debussy was very excited by the foreign music he heard at the Paris World's Fair. Perhaps you can read more about that event and find out what else was new and exciting there.

RAVEL

Listen to Ravel's *Bolero* and tell what you think of it. Do you like the repetition or does it bother you? Why is the repetition not really repetition?

Draw a picture to illustrate a Mother Goose Nursery Rhyme which Ravel might have used in his *Ma Mere L'Oye*.

Impressionism

Complete the following sentences by circling the correct word.

1. Impressionistic music is (hazy, definite)
2. The main instrument of impressionism is (the piano, the harp)
3. An impressionistic composer is (Chopin, Ravel)
4. An impressionist painter is (Monet, Leonardo da Vinci)
5. (Italy, France) is the country where the impressionistic movement began
6. The *Bolero* was written by (Brahms, Ravel)

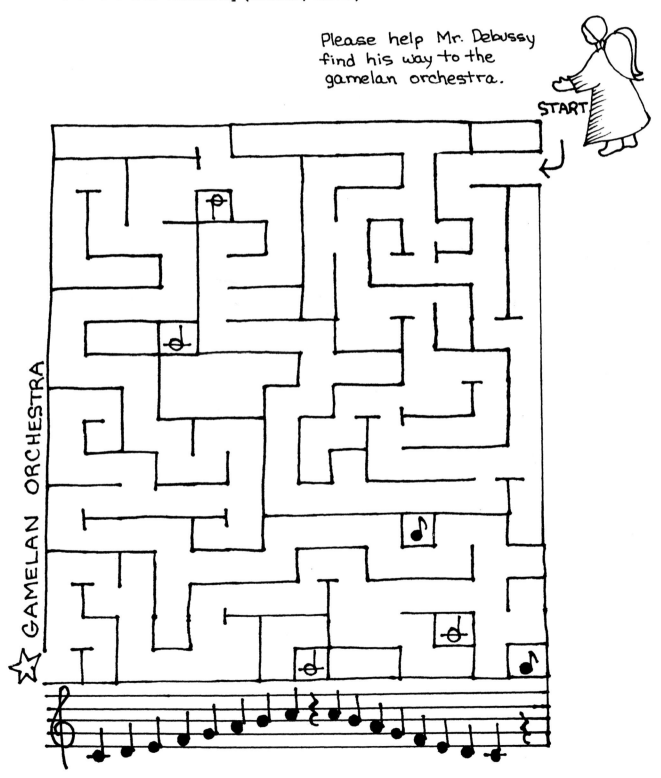

Summary

Write what you have learned about this period.

Write what you have learned about one of the composers of this period.

Modern Composers

Prokofiev
Stravinsky

and other people
of their time:

_____

_____

_____

_____

In the news!

Modernism

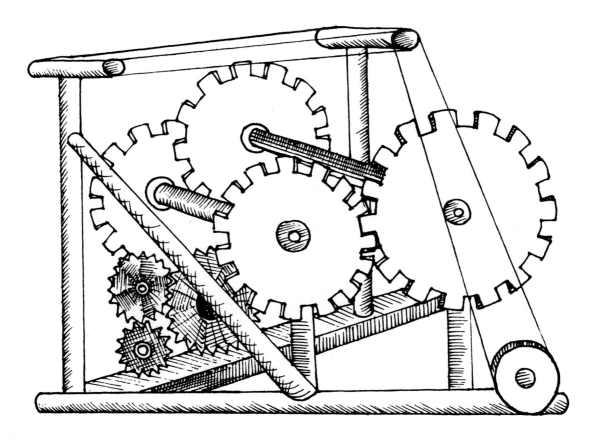

Have you noticed how each new musical period rebels against the one before it? For example, the classical period was very neat and orderly and followed strict rules of composition. After it came the emotional, romantic period, full of feelings and strong contrasts of sounds, paying little or no attention to clear-cut forms.

Now we come to another period, Twentieth Century Modernism, which turns its back on the dreamy, vague hazy music of the Impressionistic period. This new period, with its harsh **dissonance**, savage rhythms and clashing chords, replaced the lovely floating harmonies and delicate, gentle sounding chords of impressionism. This new music showed strong influences of the industrial age and sounds of the steel mills.

Two outstanding composers of this dissonant, modern music are Igor Stravinsky and Sergei Prokofiev. both Russian-born men. Let's meet them and get to know something about their music.

dissonance: sounds which are not pleasing to the ear, not harmonic.

Percussion

The percussion instruments, which produce sound by being struck or shaken, are by far the oldest instruments known. Do you remember in one of the first sections of our book (the "When" of music) we mentioned that cavemen used to clap wooden blocks together to send messages? Since the beginning of time man has used a form of drum, (skin stretched over a hollow piece of wood) to communicate. Today people still are moved to excitement by the stirring roll of drums or the clang of one metal on another.

The number of percussion instruments (such as the large kettle drums, the glockenspiel, xylophone, the celesta and the chimes) has increased, but the principles of the construction have not. Some, such as the glockenspiel and xylophone, produce sounds of **definite pitch.** Those that produce sounds of **indefinite pitch** are the snare drums, bass drum, the tambourine, cymbals and gong.

These percussion instruments were very popular with composers like Stravinsky, and other modern composers, who wanted to produce wild and primitive sounds in their music.

Sergei Prokofiev 1881 - 1953

How many of you remember what a child prodigy is? And how many of you can name the greatest of all musical prodigies whom we have met? Well if you answered a child musical genius to the first question, and Mozart to the second, you would have answered both correctly. Sergei Prokofiev, the great Russian pianist and composer has often been compared to Mozart. When he was only five years old, he had completed some piano pieces without even taking music lessons. When he was only twelve, little Sergei had composed a symphony, three operas and many more piano pieces. Can you imagine having so much talent! Later he went on to the famous Saint Petersburg Conservatory (who elso was a student there?) and studied composition and piano very seriously. After a brief tour of the United States, Prokofiev returned to Europe to live in Paris, France until 1933. Then he went back to Russia to compose great music for the people of his homeland.

Suggested listening: The opera *The Love of Three Oranges*, The March

Prokofiev's Music

Prokofiev composed music which represented the world he lived in, the industrial world, the world of shrieking factory whistles, blinking neon lights, masses of working men, improved means of transportation. All of these influences led him to write a ballet which glorified Russia's development of this industrial world. It was called the *Age of Steel (Le Pas d'Acier)*. It was full of all the dissonant sounds, sudden changes of harmony and energetic rhythms so typical of this modern music. During his first visit to America, he also wrote an opera called the *Love of Three Oranges* which was full of sparkle and wit. However, had he never written anything except *Peter and the Wolf*, Prokofiev would always be remembered as the composer who gave us the greatest musical present of all. He wanted to introduce children to the wonderful world of musical instruments in an interesting way. This is a simple fairytale for a narrator and an orchestra, telling the story of a Russian boy named Peter who captures a wolf and drags it off to the zoo. Each character in the story is represented by a different musical instrument. Peter is represented by the string quartet, a bird by the flute, a cat by the clarinet, a duck by the oboe, the grandfather by the bassoon and the wolf by three French horns.

Suggested listening: *Peter and the Wolf*

Igor Stravinsky 1882 - 1973

How many of you remember the great Russian composer, Rimsky-Korsakov? Had it not been for him, perhaps Igor Stravinsky, the son of a Russian opera singer, might never have left the study of law to follow a career in music. His musical parents sent young Igor to the University of St. Petersburg, and while there, he studied music along with law. He also became great friends with the youngest son of Rimsky-Korsakov and through him met the famed composer. Korsakov encouraged Stravinsky to continue with his music, and became his teacher. Although he studied law, Stravinsky settled on a career in music.

He lived in Paris for a long time, but after a trip to the U.S. in 1939 he decided to stay on in America, and he became an American citizen in 1945.

He and his family settled in Hollywood, California. He had many friends who were poets and artists and musicians, and they visited Stravinsky frequently. His family was very close to him, and he had much happiness and success during his life.

In 1942 he accepted an assignment to write a *Circus Polka* for Ringling Brothers Circus, composed for a young elephant. This was one of the most delightful experiences of his musical career. Can you think of anything that could be more fun than being involved with the circus?

Stravinsky's Music

Have you heard of the famous director of the Russian Ballet (Ballet Russe) Diaghilev? He attended a concert in St. Petersburg and heard two of Stravinsky's works, one called *Feu d'Artifice (Fireworks)*. This was written as a wedding gift for Rimsky-Korsakov's daughter. Diaghilev, who wanted to present to the Western world fine examples of Russian ballet, recognized Stravinsky's talents and asked him to write music for the Ballet Russe. His first assignment was to write the score for a ballet about *The Firebird*, which caused a real excitement when it was first heard. It was filled with many of the sounds of the new music: harsh dissonances, strange rhythms, noisy orchestration—totally different from the gentle, misty music of the impressionists.

Two other Ballets, *Petrouchka* and *The Rite of Spring,* illustrate even more clearly this new music, with barbaric dances, primitive melodies repeated over and over, and sudden shattering uses of percussion instruments.

In the *Rite of Spring* you can probably identify some of the primitive sounds which are so different from those of *Afternoon of a Fawn* by Debussy.

Suggested listening: *Rite of Spring,* "Dance of the Adolescents"

Activities

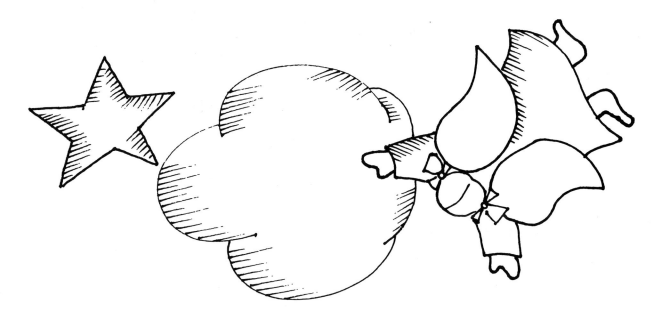

PROKOFIEV

Draw your version of *Peter and the Wolf.* You might want to do it cartoon style.

STRAVINSKY

Listen to Stravinsky's *Rite of Spring* and think of words to describe this very modern composition.

Modern

Complete the words –

1. A modern composer is S_ _ _ V_ _ _ _ _.
2. Love of *Three Oranges* was written by _ _ _ K _ _ _ _ E _.
3. Stravinsky wrote The _ _ _ _ _ _ _ _.
4. His music was filled with P _ _ _ _ _ T _ _ _ _ sounds.
5. Prokofiev was a child _ _ _ D _ _ Y.
6. Stravinsky was asked to write a ballet for D _ _ _ _ H _ _ _ _ _.
7. P_ _ _ _ _ and _ _ _ _ W _ _ _ _ was written by _ _ _ K _ _ _ _ _ _.
8. _ _ L _ _ _ Has dancing as well as music.
9. Stravinsky remained in The U _ _ _ _ _ _ S _ _ _ _ _ _.
10. Prokofiev returned to his native _ _ _ _ _ _ A.

_____

_____

_____

Summary

Write what you have learned about this period.

_____
_____
_____
_____
_____
_____
_____
_____
_____
_____

_____
_____
_____
_____
_____
_____
_____
_____

Write what you have learned about one of the composers of this period.

Ragtime, Blues, & Jazz

Scott Joplin
W. C. Handy
Louis Armstrong

and other people of their time:

_____

_____

_____

_____

Jazz, etc.

Have you ever heard music that made you want to clap yours hands, tap your feet, sway from side to side? Music that sounded so bright and brassy that you couldn't sit still? If so, chances are you were listening to a kind of music called **Jazz.**

Jazz, which began about the turn of the century, had its roots among the black people in centuries-old African tribal chants – in work songs and field hollers and spirituals among the slaves on the plantations– in sad blues songs and bouncy ragtime – and in Voodoo dances in Congo Square in New Orleans, Louisiana. That is the city credited with being the birthplace of jazz.

Jazz is mainly improvised – that is, the music is composed or played "on the spot." Originally it was not written down like Schubert's songs or Beethoven' symphonies. Instead, groups of musicians simply met together and played music as they felt it. Therefore, no jazz pieces are ever played exactly the same way twice. Thanks to the fine recording business, a performing jazz group can be taped or recorded so that we can listen to it whenever we want to.

A jazz band is smaller than the symphony orchestra which plays serious music. The main instruments are a trumpet, clarinet, cornet, bass fiddle, drums and piano. The first jazz bands included a trumpet, clarinet, trombone, bass fiddle, drums and piano.(The trumpet usually plays the melody or main tune, and the drums set the beat while the other instruments improvise.)

Jazz bands are frequently used as marching bands – in parades – or as accompaniments to black funerals, playing sad blues or spirituals on the way to the cemetery and fast, bright rhythmic pieces on the way back.

There are many funny musical terms associated with jazz such as dig (to understand), licorice stick (clarinet), cat (jazz musician) and jam (to improvise on jazz music). There are also many funny titles of jazz tunes such as "High Society," "Struttin' With Some Barbeque," "Bourbon Street Parade" and "The Muskrat Ramble."

Even funnier than jazz terms and jazz titles are the names of many of the great musicians such as Leadbelly Ledbetter, Jelly Roll Morton, Blind Lemon Jefferson and more recently, Muddy Waters. We could not possibly study about all of the many "greats" of jazz in our book but let us meet three of the most representative and popular of them: W.C. Handy, Father of the Blues; Scott Joplin, Mr. Ragtime; and Louis "Satchmo" Armstrong, Ambassador of Jazz. Each one has his own particular style, and as we listen to some of their music we shall see how they have contributed to the growth and development of jazz. Jazz is America's own music. It is of Negro origin and has been one of their greatest cultural and creative contributions.

the Trumpet

One of the most popular instruments of the jazz band is the trumpet, the instrument which jazz musicians like Louis Armstrong, King Oliver and Buddy Bolden played well. The trumpet was the featured instrument of the jazz marching bands because it lent itself so well to improvising – that is, playing a piece differently almost each time it is played – partly composing as the player went along. Also, the trumpet was loud and brassy and attracted a lot of attention. Since most trumpet players could not read music they had to play tunes by ear, and these tunes were never the same.

The trumpet is a *brass* horn which has three valves and a cup-shaped mouthpiece. Different notes are sounded by opening combinations of the valves and by adjusting the position and shaping of the mouth, tongue, and lips of the player. When a player cups his hand over the bell-shaped end of the trumpet it makes a muted, "wa-wa" sound.

The trumpet, an ancient instrument, was used in religious ceremonies and for military purposes in most of the ancient Mediterranean and Near Eastern civilizations. Because of its brilliant penetrating sounds it is frequently used today to announce or call attention to something that is going to happen. Also the trumpet is used for ceremonial occasions, such as a royal procession or military parade or review. This use is known as a fanfare.

Scott Joplin 1869 - 1917

Scott Joplin, a wandering keyboard artist, was born in Texarkana, Arkansas. Unlike many black musicians of his day, Joplin was a schooled musician, and he could read music. He learned **ragtime (syncopated** piano music which is composed not improvised) from an old German-American honky-tonk pianist. He eventually drifted to Sedalia, Missouri, a town which came to be known as the birthplace of ragtime. The reason for this was because Scott Joplin, the greatest of all ragtime composers, made this town his head-quarters. His most famous piece was the "Maple Leaf Rag" which was named after a cafe in Sedalia. It sold hundreds of thousands of copies in the first ten years of publication.

Syncopated: music with accents on normally weak or unaccented beats.

Suggested listening: "Maple Leaf Rag"

Scott Joplin's Music

Ragtime was a new style of piano music. Like the blues, it was an earlier, popular relative of jazz. However, unlike the sad, mournful sounds of the blues, ragtime was bright and happy. Also, unlike the blues, ragtime was performed by blacks and whites alike.

Ragtime was a composed or written music with a definite form, quite different, as we shall see, from the improvised music of jazz. The left hand kept a steady beat while the right hand livened up the melody with runs and **syncopations** (accenting notes in unexpected places). One of the greatest of all ragtime pieces is Scott Joplin's "Maple Leaf Rag." This piece earned him the title, "King of Ragtime." He also wrote the "Peachtree Rag," "The Strenuous Life" and one opera, *Tremonisha*, which is still performed. Interest in ragtime was renewed during 1973 due to a very popular movie called *The Sting*. Throughout the movie Scott Joplin's "rags" set the mood for the movie, and his piece "The Entertainer" became very popular once again.

Suggested listening: "The Entertainer"

W. C. Handy 1873 - 1958

When he was a very little boy in his hometown of Florence, Ala., W. C. Handy wanted to play music. The happiest hour of his day in school was the singing class. He loved the wonderful Negro spirituals (type of hymn which we will read about later) sung in the church where his father was the minister. He often made music himself by humming through a comb wrapped in tissue.

Because his family was quite poor, he worked very hard at many odd jobs. He gave his parents part of his earnings but saved a portion for himself. He desperately wanted to buy a guitar which he had seen in a store window in Florence. Finally, when he had saved enough money, he rushed out and bought the guitar. He ran home, with such pride, to show it to his father. Well, instead of being pleased, his father, the minister, was very displeased. He thought that the guitar was a sinful instrument and that any music, other than that of the church, was sinful, too. Poor little William! He was forced to take the guitar back and exchange it for, of all things, a dictionary.

Even though William tried very hard to follow his father's wishes about becoming a minister, he could never give up his dream of writing and playing music. One day, when a circus came to Florence, the cornet player in the band offered to sell William his old cornet. This was a turning point in his life. He began to play with the Florence band. From then on William stayed with music through good times and bad, playing in parades, and on river boats, and finally forming his own band and publishing company.

Although he became blind, he still loved the music he continued to write and play and was so proud of being called "Father of the Blues."

W. C. Handy's Music

The "Father of the Blues," the first man to write down and publish the blues, left us a real treasure chest of wonderful music. But just exactly what are the **blues**? Genuine blues are folk songs, with no known composer. They are usually very sad songs sung by the unsophisticated black people of the South about being without love or money or jobs or homes. However, they often have a funny thought or note of optimism or hope which makes people laugh. They follow a rhythmic pattern and, when sung, have some notes which are flattened or slurred. The blues came before jazz by quite a few years, but lent themselves to the improvisation of the jazz musicians.

Two of Handy's greatest Blues Songs are "St. Louis Blues" and "Memphis Blues." The latter was written to entertain the voters during a mayoralty campaign in Memphis, Tennessee. Later he changed the words and published it as "The Memphis Blues." His most famous, "The St. Louis Blues," written in a tango rhythm (Spanish dance rhythm which was popular then), was inspired by a phrase he heard sung in the street, "my man's got a heart like a rock cast in the sea."

When you listen to these pieces see if you can hear any flattened notes or "blues" notes and if you can feel the sadness in the words and music.

Suggested listening: "Memphis Blues" or "St. Louis Blues"

Louis Armstrong 1900 - 1972

Known as "Satchelmouth" or "Satchmo" because of his large mouth, Louis Armstrong was born in New Orleans in 1900. He is the only person we shall meet in our book who is a performer and not known as a composer. Yet, he was a special kind of composer, one called an improviser. An improviser is one who composes or arranges music while it is being played. We should know something about him and the music he played with such brilliance and excitement, because he has done so much to spread jazz to every corner of the earth. He is called the Ambassador of Jazz.

Louis, who learned to play the cornet in a Home for Boys in New Orleans, struggled all of his early years against poverty and hard times. When he was only twelve he fired a gun, which was against the law, to celebrate New Year's Eve. The police took him to jail and then to the Home for Boys, a kind of reform school for troublesome boys. However, for Louis this was a good move, as it was here that he learned to read music and to play the cornet.

Later in life, with his gravelly voice, his superb talent for blowing a horn, and his grand feeling for rhythm, he was in demand by many band leaders. He played with jazz greats such as Kid Ory and Fate Marable's band on the steamboat *Sydney* on the Mississippi River. He traveled between New Orleans and St. Louis. He became so well known that Joe "King" Oliver (leader of a great jazz band) sent for him to come to play with his group in Chicago. The rest is history.

As jazz became a household word, thanks to the recording business, its popularity spread everywhere, and Louis Armstrong's along with it. He soon had his own band and played all over the world. He even played himself in several movies. Once he came back to New Orleans and was honored as King of Zulu, the legendary black Mardi Gras parade. He visited the Boys' Home, and there he found his first old battered cornet.

His big wide grin and his famous "scat" singing were known everywhere. When he celebrated his 70th birthday in California, two years before he died, thousands of jazz lovers from all over the world came to pay tribute. One speaker after another praised him, pointing out that jazz had become popular mainly because "Satchmo" made listening to it such fun, that almost all jazz musicians copied something from him, even his "scat" singing — and that his warmth and friendliness made him one of the best loved people in show business.

Scat: Scat singing is vocal jazz when the singer invents nonsense phrases to go with the melody.

Suggested listening: any Louis Armstrong recording

Activities

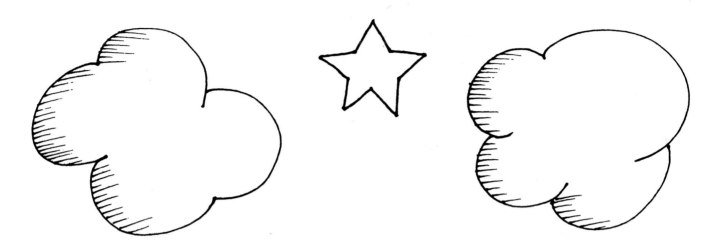

HANDY

Draw a picture of the instrument that Handy bought for himself. Then draw a picture of the item his father made him buy instead.

Tell in your own words what you think the conversation between them might have been when this occurred.

JOPLIN

Listen to a piece of Ragtime music by Joplin and list the words which describe this kind of music.

ARMSTRONG

How do you suppose Louis Armstrong felt when he was asked to be king of a carnival parade in his native city?

Jazz

T or F

1. __ Jazz bands played at funerals
2. __ W. C. Handy was Mr. Ragtime
3. __ Louis Armstrong wrote "St. Louis Blues"
4. __ A violin was an instrument in a jazz band
5. __ Improvise means to play music "on the spot"

Match

Father of Blues	New Orleans
Mr. Ragtime	Louis Armstrong
Ambassador of jazz	Sedalia, Mo.
Birthplace of jazz	Scott Joplin
Home of ragtime	W. C. Handy

Summary

Write what you have learned about this period.

Write what you have learned about one of the composers of this period.

American Composers

Stephen Foster
John P. Sousa
Irving Berlin
George Gershwin
Aaron Copland
Richard Rodgers

and other people
of their time:

_____
_____
_____

American Music

Imagine, if you can, being on a crowded, uncomfortable ship for about three months. You have left your homeland and are with people from many different countries. You are going to make a new life in a strange new world. Your main reason for leaving home is to be able to follow whatever religion you choose. Finally your ship sails into a cove where the woods meet the water's edge. At last you put your feet on dry land. But how strange it is. There is no sound except the water lapping on the shore and the wind rustling through the trees. There are no homes, no stores, no churches, no people — nothing but forest and water — no automobiles, no movies, no stereos, no TV's. Can you possibly believe that a place like that existed? Well, it did, and that's exactly the kind of place the Pilgrims found when they landed at Plymouth Rock. They had found a place with freedom to worship, but it was going to be a very hard life. They were pioneers, and pioneer living meant starting "from scratch." Before they could have cabins to sleep in, they had to cut down trees to get lumber to build them. In order to have food, they had to plant seeds and grow crops. They had to face the Indians and protect themselves from the unfriendly tribes. They were so busy just existing that they did not have time to enjoy music solely for entertainment. This was the same time in history as the Baroque Era in Europe. (Do you remember any people during that period?) The only music the Puritans sang or listened to was sacred music. The singing which was permitted was psalm-singing in unison. That was the first and only music in New England for a long time. In fact one of the songs of the early settlers which is still sung today is the "Old Hundredth," **The Doxology**.

By the year 1770, when Beethoven was born in Germany, the earliest singing schools were flourishing in New England. As our country grew and more people came to settle in the new world, music became more important in their lives. These new colonists, during the 18th century, brought with them much of the European music of Bach, Handel, Haydn and Mozart. They also brought their own musical instruments which they could play.

During the 18th century, **secular** (non religious) music became important. Businessmen in cities along the east coast began to make money and had more leisure time to enjoy music just "for the fun of it."

In the 19th century much patriotic and nationalistic (remember?) music was written. During the War of 1812 the words to our national anthem, the "Star Spangled Banner," were written by Frances Scott Key. (It did not officially become our national anthem until 1936.)

In the South the greatest contribution to American popular music was folk music from the black population. These unwilling settlers, slaves really, brought with them their love of music and inborn sense of melody and rhythm. They had their own Sunday church services, and from these came forth a new type of African-American song called the "spiritual." This was a religious song telling a story and having strong rhythms. Sometimes the black people transferred the Bible Stories into their own experience.

They also had songs that were not religious. They found that their work songs made their hard physical labor move a little more quickly. They had songs for any situation or experience and had music for pure entertainment as well.

The appealing sound and spirit of the African-American music was so popular that it was imitated on the stage of towns and cities. This light entertainment was called a minstrel show. In these shows white entertainers blackened their faces with burnt cork, sang happy and sad songs, danced, told jokes, and sang songs which poked fun at American life. The first American composer we shall meet, Stephen Foster, saw this type of show—minstrel show—in Pittsburgh when he was quite young. His music was greatly influenced by the black man's songs and the minstrel's. Our next composer of purely American music is John Philip Sousa, the March King. After Sousa we will get to know one of the best-loved composers of popular songs—Irving Berlin, and shall see how ragtime (remember?) influenced his music. Our fourth American will be George Gershwin, considered by many to be the greatest American composer—one strongly influenced by jazz and classical music as well.

Born two years after Gershwin, Aaron Copland, another American (and a great classical composer) shows the influence of Gershwin and jazz.

Another field of American music, which was becoming very popular about the time of George Gershwin, was called **musical theater** or just plain "musicals." Two of the important men in this field whom we shall learn something about are Richard Rogers and Oscar Hammerstein II.

Stephen Collins Foster 1826 - 1864

Stephen Foster was born in Pittsburgh on a very special day—July 4th, 1826—the same day our country celebrated it's fiftieth birthday. The ninth of ten children, he showed a deep love for music, against his father's wishes, even as a small child. His nurse, Lieve, often took him to her church where he heard the black people sing their stirring spirituals. Later in life, he would go down to the river and listen to the Negroes singing work songs as they loaded and unloaded the river boats. When he was older, he went to see and hear the minstrels. These spirituals, work songs, and folk songs were about all the music young Stephen knew. Since there were no records or stereos or radios or concerts, wherever was he going to hear any other music such as Beethoven or Chopin composed?

Eventually young Stephen went to Cincinnati and New York and gained fame by writing songs which were used in the minstrel shows.

He returned to Pittsburgh and married Jane McDowell. After a short year spent in New York, the Fosters returned again to Pittsburgh and real trouble began. Stephen, unfortunately, was no business man and did not know how to make much money from his songs. His wife left him, and he began to drink too much. It is sad to think that a man who could write such fine songs as "Camptown Races" and such beautiful songs as "My Old Kentucky Home" should die alone and poor.

Stephen Foster's Music

Stephen Foster was a true son of the United States. He sang about his own land and his own people. His songs had simple melodies and words and the sincere quality of folk songs. The sentiments expressed in his music – friendship, love, loyalty and home – are understood by every one.

Stephen Foster left a treasure chest of songs. His first song, "The Tioga Waltz," was written when he was only thirteen years old, and at sixteen, he had his first published song, "Open thy Lattice, Love." By the time he was twenty, he had composed many songs for the minstrel shows, including "Old Uncle Ned," "Oh! Susanna," and "Old Folks at Home," which the Christy Minstrels were the first to sing. The publisher made lots of money, but alas, not poor Stephen!

He wrote a song for his pet dog called "Old Dog Tray." "The Glendy Burke," "Jeannie with the Light Brown Hair," "Massa's in Der Cold, Cold Ground" and "Beautiful Dreamer" are amongst his best-loved songs, too numerous to mention all of them.

Suggested listening: Songs of Stephen Foster

John Philip Sousa 1854 - 1932

Born in Washington, D.C. (our nation's capitol) John Philip Sousa heard a lot of band music. It was a great time to hear bands, during the Civil War, for patriotic feelings are most stirred up in time of war. Young Philip loved it all, good or bad. His father had played a trombone in the Marine Band, and he wanted to follow in his father's footsteps. When he was a little boy he began his musical training studying the violin, and when he was about thirteen, he was offered a place in a circus band. Just think how appealing that idea would be to any boy! Well, it certainly was for Philip, but not for his father, who had other ideas for him. Not having enough money to send his son to study in Europe, he enlisted young Sousa in the Marine Corps, as an apprentice, to study music. After many years of working and performing and composing, he became the leader of the Marine Band. He held this job for twelve years and then asked to be released to form his own band. He made several tours of Europe and once around the world. He was so well received that a little British brass band newspaper ran an article calling him the "March King" and saying that he had done for marches what the "Waltz King" (remember him?) had done for waltzes.

Sousa's Music

During his long, busy, happy life, Sousa wrote over a hundred marches, besides some waltzes, operas, and songs. However, it is for his very bright, brassy, joyous marches that he is best remembered. The melodies are singable and the rhythms so lively that they make even a weary marcher want to "keep moving." He even had an instrument maker change the shape of the tuba (the big brass horn) so that the large bell-shaped end would be turned out to spread the sound. The coils were even changed so that it could be worn over the shoulder. This new instrument is called the **Sousaphone**.

Among his most famous marches are the "Washington Post" and "The Stars and Stripes." These are often played during parades, sports events, when ships depart, at White House receptions when foreign dignitaries (important people) visit, and for band concerts. His "Semper Fidelis" is the official Marine Corps theme song.

Suggested listening: "Semper Fidelis" or other marches.

Irving Berlin 1888 - 1989

Born in Russia, the youngest of eight children, Izzy Baline (later Irving Berlin) and his family came to the United States in 1892, when he was just four years old. His father had been a rabbi, and when the Jews were persecuted (very badly treated) the Balines fled the country and crossed the ocean to come to America. They settled in a ghetto of New York City. Soon each member of the family, except little Izzy (who was too young), went out to help earn a living. Izzy tried to find odd jobs to help at home, but he could not contribute enough. He felt that he was a burden. Finally, when he was only thirteen years old, he did something which changed not only his life and his family's fortune, but in a large measure changed the music in America as well. He ran away from home, determined to pursue his musical interests.

He sold newspapers on street corners, began his musical career as a singing waiter and finally was given a job with a publishing company writing lyrics (words) to music. He composed many songs, even though he could not read music. His first published song in 1911, "Alexander's Ragtime Band," was a huge hit, and from there he went on to fame and fortune.

He was a good son, and after he had made a lot of money, he brought his mother and brothers and sisters uptown to a beautiful, fine house which he had fixed up just for them. He was also awarded, in 1955, a medal by President Eisenhower for his contribution in composing patriotic songs. That is quite an accomplishment for someone who started off as a poor little immigrant, isn't it?

Irving Berlin's Music

It is amazing that a person like Irving Berlin, who could not read a note of music, was able to create both the words and music to nine hundred songs. (Can you remember the name of another great song writer from the Romantic period who wrote over six hundred songs?) Irving was greatly influenced by the syncopated rhythms of ragtime (so clearly seen in "Alexander's Ragtime Band") and by the bouncy beat of jazz. He wrote for Broadway musical shows and motion pictures as well. *Annie Get Your Gun* is one which was first a musical and then a movie.

While he was in the army, he wrote and produced two all-soldier shows. The song "Oh, How I Hate to Get Up In The Morning" is from one of them.

He will probably best be remembered for three songs which have truly become classics: "God Bless America," "White Christmas" and "Easter Parade."

Suggested listening: "White Christmas"
"Easter Parade"
"God Bless America"

George Gershwin 1898 - 1937

As a young boy in New York City, George Gershwin had no interest in music whatsoever — or for that matter in school or reading either. He loved sports, particularly baseball, and thought that boys who took music lessons were "sissies," or "little Maggies" as he called them. However, when he did discover music through the violinist Max Rosen, the two became friends, and a whole new world opened up for George. He studied composition, took piano lessons, and became a song plugger, (pianist who plays songs of hopeful composers) in **Tin Pan Alley.** He also read all he could about the great musical personalities and learned to play many instruments so that he might further his knowledge of orchestration. George composed music frantically, almost as though he knew his life would be short and he had so much he wanted to accomplish.

He never married but had many friends, both men and women. He had a wonderfully close relationship with his family. He and his brother Ira wrote many songs and shows together. He even wrote an opera, *Porgy and Bess;* but not long after it was written he became ill in Hollywood with severe headaches and died a few weeks later. In his short life of thirty-nine years he left a tremendous amount of the most wonderful music the world has ever heard. Gershwin achieved everything he could with music — this same man who, as a boy, turned up his nose at the little "maggies" and wanted no part of anything as sissy as studying music.

Tin Pan Alley: this was the nickname for the place where publishing companies had song pluggers perform their new music. In the days before radios or stereos were common, how else could music be heard?

Gershwin's Music

George Gershwin loved jazz and felt that it was truly American music. All of his music, both popular and serious, contains threads of jazz and blues. His first big hit "Swannee" (not to be confused with Stephens Foster's "Way Down Upon the Swanee River") sold millions of copies. He was only twenty-six when Paul Whiteman, a leading jazz band leader, asked him to write a serious symphonic work using the jazz style. Gershwin too had always wanted to make jazz the basis of a serious piece of music. The result was the wealth of melody and rhythm known as "Rhapsody in Blue." In 1924 he crossed the barrier between Tin Pan Alley and Carnegie Hall when he played his *Concerto in F* with the New York Symphony Orchestra. The "American in Paris" is another classical jazz favorite.

His popular songs all contain blues, ragtime and jazz. Some of his most memorable ones are "The Man I Love," "Embraceable You," "Fascinating Rhythm" and "'S Wonderful."

He wrote the music for musicals, among them *Strike Up the Band* and *Of Thee I Sing*. His highly successful folk opera *Porgy and Bess,* is often called the greatest American opera.

Suggested listening: "Rhapsody in Blue"

Selections from *Porgy and Bess*

Aaron Copland 1900 - 1990

Aaron Copland is the realization of the great American dream. The son of poor Russian Jewish immigrants, who settled in Brooklyn and worked very, very hard to build up a prosperous business, he was able to pursue a successful career in music. His parents, (whose name Kaplan was mispronounced by immigration officials and changed to Copland) taught him the importance of devotion to duty and saving money. Because of this training he was able to study piano and harmony in New York and was one of the first American students to go to Paris to study. A life of music was against his hard-working businessman father's ambitions but thanks to an understanding mother, Aaron was able to pursue HIS dream.

While in Paris he studied under the great teacher and organist, Mlle. Nadia Boulanger, for whom he wrote a symphony. This organ symphony brought him fame and recognition in America. He was even awarded a Guggenheim Fellowship, which helped him to be financially independent, as he did not want to take money from his parents.

Aaron Copland has taught, studied, and composed at Tanglewood in Massachusetts, in Mexico City, Mexico, and in Hollywood, California as well as New York and Paris. He has been well received everywhere and is considered the Dean of American Music.

Aaron Copland's Music

How many of you know the cowboy songs "O Bury Me Not on the Lone Prairie", or "Goodbye, Old Paint"? Have you ever sung them? Can you imagine them being included in a classical work such as a ballet? Well, Aaron Copland's ballet *Billy the Kid* is filled with these folk tunes as well as many others and two more of his ballets, *Rodeo,* and *Appalachian Spring,* are based on such American classics. A truly American composer, he tends to use folk music in as many ways as possible, and his *Lincoln Portrait* even employs songs of Stephen Foster. (Remember him?) During the 1920's some of his serious music began to show the influence of jazz, which was gaining in popularity and respectability. He heard, in 1924, the now-famous "First American Jazz Concert" conducted by Paul Whiteman (remember him?) introducing George Gershwin's *Rhapsody in Blue.*

Copland was very anxious to write music which would appeal to young people as he felt that the youth of today would be the adult audience of tomorrow. He composed his first opera, *The Second Hurrricane,* and an orchestral work, *An Outdoor Overture,* which were to be performed by school children.

Fortunately for Copland (who was anxious to see that the music of his fellow-composers could be heard by many people), the radio was a very popular piece of equipment, and many people had them in their homes. Thus, thousands of people could hear a performance of a great piece of music. Also, the movie industry was growing and improving, and he composed several motion picture scores, including *Our Town.* Today, as television has become a household word, just imagine how many people can see Copland's ballets being performed or watch a symphony orchestra play any of his works.

Suggested listening: *Billy the Kid,* "The Card Game", "The Fight"
Appalachian Spring, "The Celebration"

Richard Rodgers 1902 - 1979

Richard Rodgers was born in New York. His father was a doctor, and his mother was an accomplished amateur pianist. They often went to the theater to see stage shows and brought home entire scores (words and music) of the operettas and musicals which they had seen. As a result there was always lots of singing and music in the Rodgers' home. By the time he was four, young Richard could pick out, on the piano, many "show" tunes. He composed his first song at fourteen, and at fifteen wrote his first complete musical score. The next year he met a man who would change his life and further the growth of American music. The man, named Lorenz Hart, was a great **lyricist**, but he was also quite moody, sloppy in appearance, and very much against the "establishment", just the opposite of Richard Rodgers. In spite of these differences the two became a team, known as Rodgers and Hart, and together wrote such great musicals as *A Connecticut Yankee, The Girl Friend* and *Pal Joey.* They even went to Hollywood and wrote for the movies but did not like it out there and were happy to return to Broadway.

After Hart died, Rodgers teamed up with another great lyricist, Oscar Hammerstein II, and together Rodgers and Hammerstein wrote and produced eight of the most popular musicals of all time, as well as the beloved movie *State Fair.*

Rodgers and Hammerstein have done so much for musical theater both in writing shows and producing them that their names have become legendary, as those of Gilbert and Sullivan.

lyricist: one who writes the words for a song

Rodgers and Hammerstein's Music

People milling all around – talking, laughing, checking the time – eagerly awaiting the curtain call when suddenly a bell rings, signalling everyone to their seats – a frenzied rush down the aisles, a second bell rings – the house lights dim and all is quiet as the audience settles down to listen to the orchestra begin the overture (music played before the curtin goes up on a musical). Then, as it is finishing, the curtains open and the show begins. It's a wonderful feeling – this anticipation of the evening's entertainment. If any of you have ever been to the theater to see a show then you know what it's like.

For years Richard Rodgers' music and Oscar Hammerstein's lyrics have provided audiences the world over with this exciting kind of entertainment which is known as musical comedy. It combines a plot (story), talking, singing, dancing, costumes and scenery. All of these ingredients are found in their first great show (1943) *Oklahoma,* one of the most successful musical comedies of all time. It is a completely American show. The characters are farm hands wearing overalls and farm girls in aprons. The music is in folk style and suited to the midwestern setting, the State of Oklahoma. Almost every year since it opened *Oklahoma* has been produced somewhere on stage and has even been made into a movie.

Among their other musical shows which have proven what a successful team Rodgers and Hammerstein have been are *South Pacific, The King and I,* and their favorite work *Carousel.*

Suggested listening: *Oklahoma, Carousel*

Activities

FOSTER

Choose a Stephen Foster song and draw a picture which the title suggests. See if others can guess which song you have illustratedd.

SOUSA

John Phillip Sousa, the March King! How many musical words can you make from his name and title, the March King? You may include instruments, composers, musical compositions and musical forms. (Example; sonata can be spelled. Use the glossary for ideas.

BERLIN

Draw a funny or outlandish hat for a girl or boy to wear in the Easter Parade.

GERSHWIN

Gershwin's *American in Paris* is a piece of music filled with sounds associated with Paris. What are some sounds which would inspire a composer writing a composition about the place where you live?

RODGERS

Do you know any of the stories of Rodgers and Hammerstein's musicals? Ask your parents if they have a favorite.

COPLAND

Draw a scene which pictures one of the episodes you have heard from *Billy the Kid*.

G	E	R	S	H	W	I	N	B	D
O	F	O	S	T	E	R	I	N	G
K	♪	D	S	O	N	G	A	I	M
L	E	G	O	T	U	B	A	T	A
A	M	E	S	U	O	S	C	A	R
H	I	R	V	I	N	G	♪	G	C
O	T	S	T	E	P	H	E	N	H
M	U	S	I	C	●	O	♪	I	E
A	P	I	A	N	O	R	G	S	S
S	H	O	W	T	I	N	A	P	T
O	I	L	E	S	U	O	R	A	C

Circle the words in the above "seek and find" puzzle

Gershwin
Stephen
Oscar
music
Oklahoma
marches
band
song
tuba
Foster
Irving
piano
show

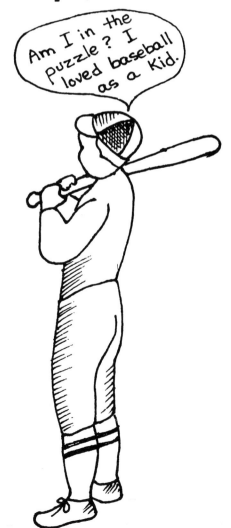

Summary

Write what you have learned about this period.

_____
_____
_____
_____
_____
_____
_____
_____
_____

_____
_____
_____
_____
_____
_____
_____
_____
_____

Write what you have learned about one of the composers of this period.

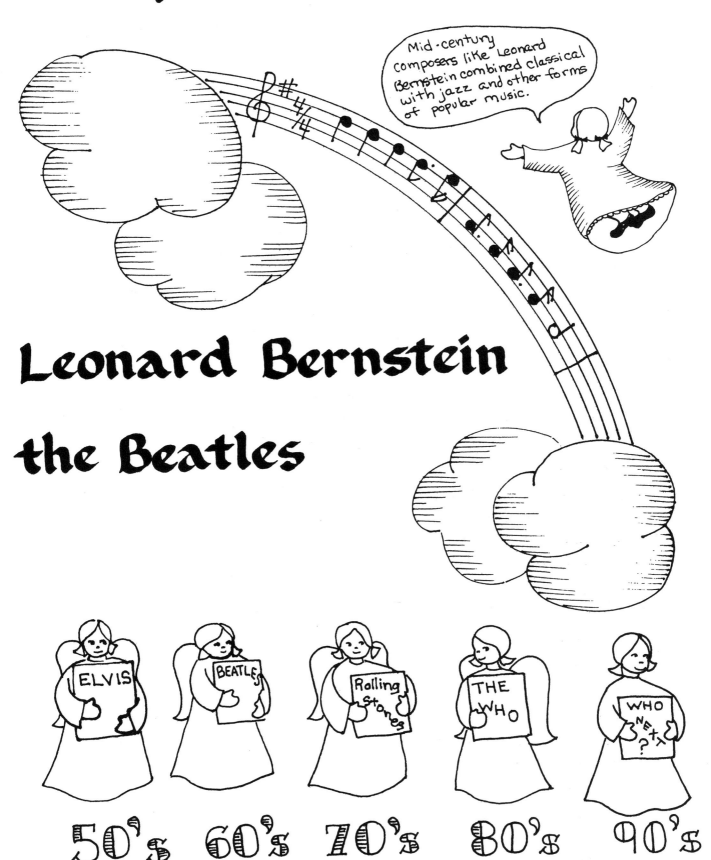

Mid-Century Music

Music today is generally called Rock, (either rock and roll, soul, rockabilly or folk-rock). This new music began about the middle of the 1950's. Just as jazz was developed in the 20's and 30's by the younger generation, so this new music was developed in the 50's and 60's by another new generation. After World War II popular songs of composers such as Irving Berlin, George Gershwin and Richard Rodgers had lost their appeal. So had the sounds of the Big Bands such as those of Glenn Miller, Tommy Dorsey, and even the great jazz artist Duke Ellington.

This "old" music and its productions has been replaced by shouting, by crackling noise, by loud amplification (increase of sound), by bright flashing lights and shiny sparkling costumes. It is the music of the young people. It is concerts in open parks, groups recording in studios, a change to the guitar and other plucked instruments from the violins and horns and piano, the use of pure volume (loudness) for its own sake.

Rock music has grown out of the white man's country and western folk music and the black people's rhythm and blues. The earliest type of rock was called rockabilly. It began in the middle 50's in Memphis, Tenn., with Elvis Presley as its leader. He was the teenage idol and earned the title "The King". In the early 60's, groups like the Beatles and other British rock groups appeared on the scene. Black rhythm and blues furthered the growth of rock. In the 70's this R & B (as it was called) influenced a great poet-singer, Bob Dylan, who sang folk-rock.

There was another influence on rock music, called "soul" music. Basically a gospel-style singing (remember gospel?) combining blues, jazz and rhythm, it had been popular with black audiences for years. Soul had its roots in black, southern rock and roll of the 50's. Artists like the singer Chuck Berry, the pianist composer "Fats" Domino, and explosive vocalist "Little" Richard were some of the big names of soul music.

Hard rock, with its throbbing, ear-splitting sounds, electronic rock, which uses synthesizers and light shows, and raga rock (rock which uses non-western instruments such as the sitar), are all developments of the new rock music. It has even incorporated the classical styles such as opera. An example is *Jesus Christ Superstar*. Soft rock, which is quieter, has now become popular with the "older" group who were teenagers in the 50's and 60's. Soft rock or folk rock singers and writers began to gain a following with artists like James Taylor, and Simon and Garfunkel.

There are far too many individuals and groups to try to mention them all, but the group we would like for you to meet is the Beatles. They have had tremendous influence on the development of rock music.

the Guitar

The guitar, a six-stringed instrument, was popular in Europe from the later part of the middle ages on. It was introduced into Spain by the Moors and was very effective in reproducing distinctive Spanish folk rhythms. By the seventeenth century, the guitar had become the national instrument of Spain. In the United States it has become a popular jazz instrument and is widely used in accompanying folk and country and western music. Perhaps it's most well-known use since the 60's has been as an electrically amplified instrument in rock and roll bands. Its sound is made louder and more penetrating by electrical impulses.

The six strings of the guitar are played by being plucked by the fingers or with a plectrum, a small piece of flexible material. The frets, narrow raised lines crossing the finger board, show the proper places for the fingers to produce different sounds or chords.

Leonard Bernstein 1918 - 1990

How many of you have ever known anyone who was a success during his or her lifetime doing five different things? Leonard Bernstein, born in Massachusetts to Russian immigrant parents, was such a person. Known as Lenny, he has become a legend in his own time as a pianist, composer, conductor, writer, and teacher. When he was only ten years old he came home from school one day and found an upright piano which had been sent to his family by his Aunt Clara. (Who else had an Aunt Clara who sent a musical instrument?) He fell in love with that heavy, bulky old instrument, and from that moment on decided that music would be his life. Like many earlier musicians he had trouble convincing his unmusical parents of his decision. (Can you name some other musicians who had this same problem?) Eventually Lenny's parents gave in, and not only did he compose and perform, but he became the youngest person ever (age twenty-five) to conduct the great New York Philharmonic Orchestra. He substituted for the famous conductor Bruno Walter. He was very frightened and nervous, but once he began to lead the musicians he forgot about being in front of a huge audience. He lost himself in the music almost as though he were a part of it, and of the orchestra as well. In 1958 he became the regular conductor of the New York Philharmonic Orchestra, a position he held for ten years, being known as its most brilliant conductor.

Bernstein's Music

Leonard Bernstein was at his happiest when conducting a symphony program for young audiences. He related well with children and began giving concerts on television especially for them. He liked sharing what he knew about music and acted like an excited enthusiastic youngster when he talked about music.

He has composed symphonies, a ballet called Fancy Free, music for motion pictures, and several musicals, the most popular of which is probably *West Side Story*. Like many twentieth century composers who combined "old" sounds and ideas and music with new rhythms and ideas and beats, Bernstein looked ahead by combining jazz elements with concert music. In this great musical, *West Side Story,* he also dealt with a serious theme (gang warfare and racial tensions in New York City slums) whereas most earlier musicals were light and happy. In one piece from *West Side Story,* "The Dance at the Gym," Bernstein used unusual rhythms and beats, and harsh, dissonant harmonies.

Suggested listening: *West Side Story,* "Dance at the Gym", "Maria"

The Beatles

Wild screaming and shrieking—girls swooning and fainting—boys stomping their feet and jumping up and down—over a hundred policemen for protection—all of this greeted the Beatles as they stepped out of their plane at Kennedy Airport for their first visit to the United States on February 7, 1964. And just who were these "Beatles"? They were the most popular rock and roll idols of teenagers in England. They came to America to appear live on TV on the Ed Sullivan Show, and over one third of the entire population of the United States tuned in. Suddenly they had taken America by storm with their *mop* hair cuts (the start of a continuing fad), collarless jackets, impish, lovable ways, poking fun at themselves, and of course with their great rock music.

They were born in Liverpool, England, a cold port city. It was here during the late 1950's that the Beatles began their musical careers. There were many sailors and seamen in Liverpool and many night clubs and bars for their entertainment. These bars employed rock and roll bands, and these four young men (who first called themselves the Silver Beatles) formed one of the bands.

Following a successful tour of Hamburg, Germany, they returned to England. They dressed in leather jackets and jeans, had long unkempt hair styles, were loud, and full of rock and roll. They were discovered by a rather elegant young man named Brian Epstein, who had a record store and music contacts. He became their manager in 1961. He cleaned them up and fitted them with their collarless jackets and ties. By 1962 they had made their debut on TV in England, and from then on Beatlemania swept not only England but the continent as well.

Following their visit to the United States the Beatles continued to grow in popularity and had one successful album after another. But alas, the end was nearing. Amid fusses and disagreements, the group separated in 1970, and each went his own way. They are continuing their separate careers (except for John Lennon who was senselessly murdered in 1980).

Seldom, if ever, has a group of performers or entertainers had such an impact on the world as the Beatles have had, and continue to have, as their music is played year in and year out.

Music of the Beatles

Before the rock music of the Beatles, the importance of commercial success (that is, making money) was the number one thought of rock composers and performers. Music that would "sell" was what producers wanted. However, the Beatles were to prove that new, different sounds could sell too. They were the first to show that pop and classical music could be brought together, borrowing sounds from Schubert and Bach and Elizabethan melodies. They even had their arranger George Martin use symphonic orchestras as a back-up accompaniment.

In the beginning the Beatles did not show any real change from standard rock'n'roll. Hits like "Shake, Rattle, and Roll" were typical rhythm and blues songs. So were their first American hits, "She Loves You" and "I Wanna Hold Your Hand". However, with the creative ability of songwriters Paul McCartney and John Lennon, they began to experiment with the musical potential of the rock style. They used unusual foreign instruments such as the Indian sitar. In "Eleanor Rigby" they used cellos, (which had not been used before, except in orchestras) to create a haunting effect. In the funny-titled album "Rubber-Soul," Ringo performed on the Hammond organ, and George Martin played **harmonium.** They advanced their style in **psychedelic rock** in "Yellow Submarine," showing that they were always moving ahead and experimenting. At the same time they had written the beautiful ballad "Yesterday" performed by a string octet (eight) reminiscent of Baroque music—and also the lovely song "Michelle".

One of the best examples of the Beatles' musical experimentation is their Sgt. Pepper's Lonely Hearts Club Band, an album produced in 1967. It is the first album of its kind, a **"song cycle"** rock album with each song relating to the next. It uses all of the devices which we have been talking about: psychedelic sounds, electronic tricks, ("Lucy in the Sky") large orchestras, and Indian instruments ("Within You, Without You").

Let's listen to the music of the Beatles and try and point out some of these musical experimentations which have made their music lasting, and have contributed so greatly to the development of yet another phase of music in general.

Harmonium: Small reed organ

Psychedelic rock—on records, unusual sounds and excessive volume; on stage, the use of flashing lights, twisted pictures, ever-changing designs.

Suggested listening: *Sgt. Pepper's Lonely Hearts Club Band* or *Best of the Beatles*

Activities

Leonard Bernstein is famous as a conductor, composer, pianist, writer and teacher. Which do you think was his favorite activity? Write a short paragraph telling why and draw a picture of him performing this activity.

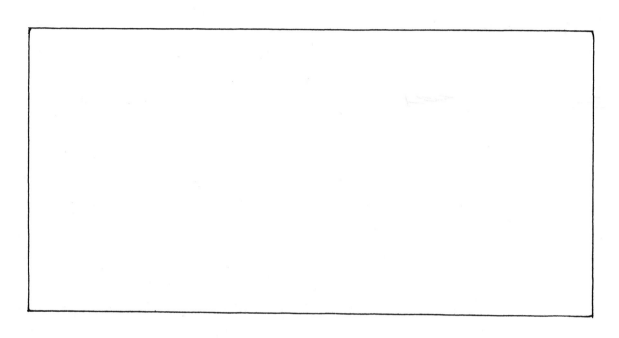

What Next?

Hopefully, *Bach to Rock* has succeeded in fullfilling its purpose for its readers – to open a door to a whole new world – a world filled with the beauty and enjoyment of music. This book is really just an introduction, a handshake between its pages and its readers, merely a brief beginning of what the author hopes will develop into a warm, close friendship.

From the fancy, ornate Baroque world of Handel and Bach to the dreamy, Impressionistic world of Debussy and Ravel, to the brassy, exciting world of Jazz, to the "now" music of the Beatles, all sorts of sounds and styles have been presented. However, there are literally hundreds, maybe even thousands, more composers that you have not met. If you have enjoyed learning about the musicians and their music in *Bach to Rock* then perhaps you will be tempted to want to find out something about **the others.**

As we have mentioned, each new period is a development or change from the one before it, and that like today new music or "different" music has taken a long time to be accepted. Just as parents have fussed and fumed over their sons and daughters adoration of the music of the Rolling Stones or the Supremes , so these same parents' parents fussed and fumed over their "swooning" over singers like Frank Sinatra in the thirties and forties. Think too, how badly they must have treated Stranvinsky and the first performance of his "new" far-out *Rite of Spring* because it sounded so different from Beethoven. Yet, there were many terrible criticisms of Beethoven's "wild, loud music" by the followers of Bach and Haydn.

What this all means is that "new" music must stand the test of time in order to be appreciated and accepted.

Music is constantly growing and changing. There is now an increase in the contribution to composition by women. Today there are even special concerts which feature the work of women composers.

The musical story is not finished yet, and what the future holds is anybody's guess. One thing is certain though, that just as in the past, composers will continue to look for new ways to express themselves musically and strive to be accepted. Hopefully people like you, the readers of *Bach to Rock*, will become more and more familiar with old and new music, will enjoy it and will open your hearts and ears and minds to each and every phase of it.

Activities

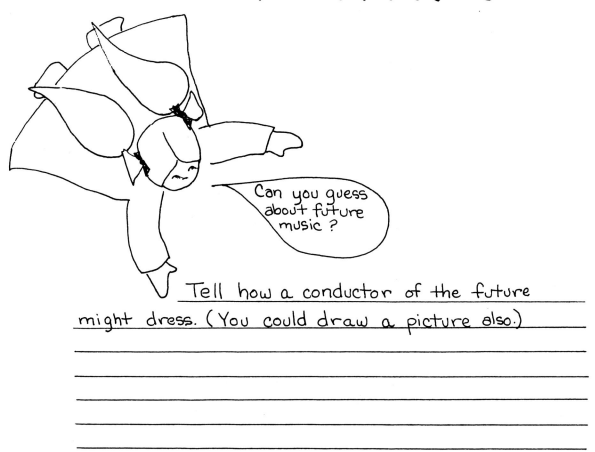

Tell how a conductor of the future might dress. (You could draw a picture also.)

_____

_____

_____

_____

_____

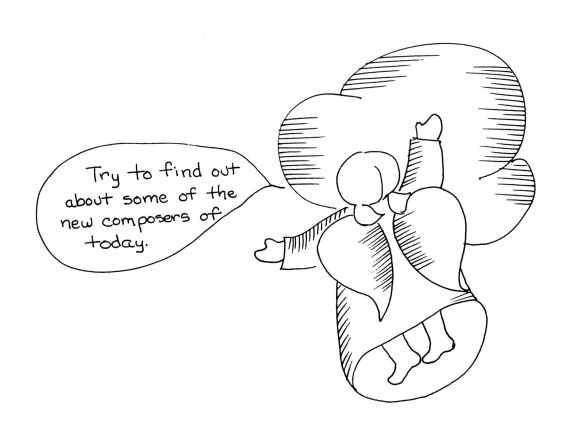

The Orchestra

The orchestra, a group of musicians performing on instruments, began to take shape at the start of the Baroque period. A composer named Claudio Monteverdi was probably the first to write music for a definite group of instruments for special parts of the composition. The growth of the orchestra, by the classical period, was dependent on the size of the hall where the music was to be performed and on the availability of the various instruments and musicians to play them. Strings were the most important instruments, but by the eighteenth century brass horns and kettle drums were added. Gradually, over the years the orchestra has grown to be the "big" symphony orchestra that we know today.

The present-day symphony orchestra is usually made of about one hundred men and women. It is divided into four sections, or families. These are know as the strings, wood-winds, brass and percussion. The largest group is the string family which keeps the melody flowing. It is the largest because the strings make softer sounds than the others and need more people to play them in order to be properly heard.

A conductor (leader of the orchestra) stands before the musicians and directs the orchestra with a baton (remember what that is?). Can you imagine what a job that must be, to lead a hundred musicians with different groups playing different music so that they all blend together and sound harmonious? It takes a really good conductor and a lot of team effort, even more than for a football coach, to lead or direct his team to victory for he only has to work with eleven players at a time.

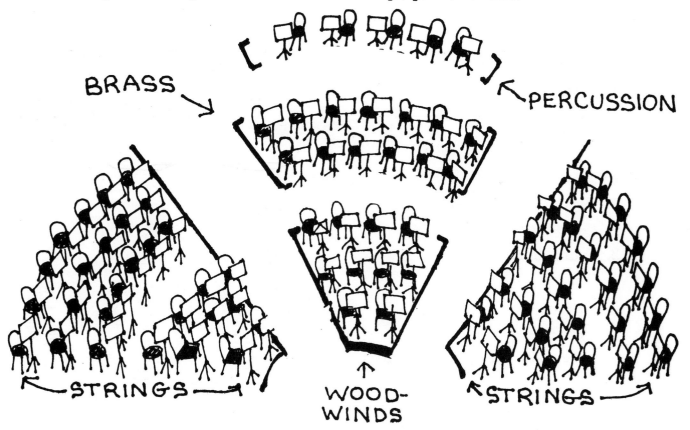

BRASS

PERCUSSION

STRINGS

WOOD-WINDS

STRINGS

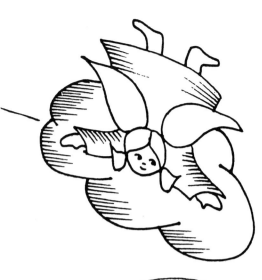

The instruments of the string family are:

1. violins
2. violas
3. cellos
4. double basses
5. harp (only used when a special part is written for it)

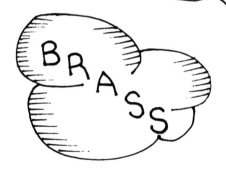

The Brass instruments are:

1. Trumpet/Cornet
2. Trombone
3. French horn
4. Tuba

The Wood-wind instruments are:

1. Piccolo
2. Flute
3. Clarinet
4. Bassoon
5. Oboe
6. English horn

The Percussion instruments are:

1. Timpani (Kettledrums)
2. Bass drum
3. Snare drum
4. Gong
5. Xylophone
6. Cymbals

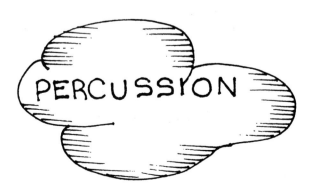

Any other instruments which are struck.

Who Am I?

I have entertained the world with my beautiful dance music. Born in Vienna, I conducted an orchestra and was given the title "The Waltz King." Who am I?

I am an Italian by birth. In the early eighteenth century I made an instrument which became very popular and important during the Romantic period. It was called the pianoforte, the earliest form of a piano. Who am I?

Although I was deaf, I composed beautiful symphonies, one which even had a chorus. My childhood was very unhappy and I was forced to practice the piano all the time. Who am I?

Born in Florence, Ala. I grew up and earned the title "Father of the Blues." This was because I composed great blues songs, the most popular being *St Louis Blues*. Who am I?

I am known as the father of the symphony and my nick-name is Papa. I had a wonderful patron named Prince Esterhazy. Who am I?

When I was a young boy I wanted to be a great piano performer. However, I damaged my finger and could not play well any more. I composed music, some especially for children and my wife Clara played it. Who am I?

I was born in Germany and wrote many operas, or music dramas. They were about super heros and I composed very dramatic music for them. The leitmotif was my invention. Who am I?

Every one loves my popular songs especially *God Bless America*, and *White Christmas* and *Easter Parade*. Who am I?

I was the youngest conductor of the New York Symphony Orchestra. As such, I was able to talk to young (as well as adult) audiences about music and help people learn to enjoy it. Who am I?

I live in a very cold country in Northern Europe. It is called Norway. I wrote music using my country's folk songs and I wrote music to accompany a Norwegian folk tale called *Peer Gynt* Who am I?

I never married and have no children but I collect children's toys. I am remembered for a very rhythmic piece with a strong Spanish feeling. It is called *Bolero.* Who am I?

Although we never met, I became great friends with my pen pal Mme VonMeck. She encouraged my music and I am probably best remembered for my ballet music for the Nutcracker Ballet. Who am I?

Although I was born in Russia. I moved to America and became an American citizen. I composed very modern music such as *"The Rite of Spring."* One of my American compositions was an elephant polka which was written for the circus. Who am I?

I composed many pieces for the organ, including the Tocatta and Fugue in D minor which sounds very spooky. I have twenty-one children. Who am I?

I was a famous singer in the 1950's. I began a kind of music in Memphis, Tenn. called Rockabilly. Who am I?

When I was a small boy, my nurse Lieve took me to her church where I first heard spirituals. Later, when I was older I went to listen to the minstrel singers. I am best remembered for songs I wrote such as *My Old Kentucky Home* , *Swanee River* and *The Glendy Burke.* Who am I?

Even though my parents were immigrants, I was born in America and always loved cowboy and western folk music. I used many of these tunes in my ballets and other "serious" music. Who am I?

Glossary

Absolute Music–   Music composed simply as music without a story or program

Ballet–   A formal dance performed usually with costumes, scenery and musical accompaniment.

Baroque–   Period in history from about 1600 to 1750, when all of the arts were very ornate and fancy

Baton–   The stick a conductor uses to beat time

Blues–   Folk songs, usually about sad subject, ending on a happy "or optimistic note . . ." Some notes are flattened or slurred for effect.

Brass Band–   Small instrumental group consisting of brass and percussion frequently used for jazz funerals

Cantata–   A work for singers and instruments with some speech-like sections, can be religious or secular–religious cantatas are shorter and less elaborate than an oratorio

Cat–   Jazz term for a jazz musician

Chamber Music–   Music written to be played in a small hall or room. Usually written for four or five instruments

Classical Period–   A time in history from about 1750 - 1800 which was very neat and orderly. Classical composers were more concerned with rules and form than expressing their feelings

Clavichord–   An early stringed keyboard instrument

Concerto–   A musical composition for solo instrument and orchestra

Dig–   Jazz term meaning to understand

Dissonance–   Sounds which are not pleasing to the ear, clashing sounds

Etude–   French word for a study or exercise—sometimes an artistic piece of music

Folk Music–   Music expressing customs, traditions and emotions of the people of a country

Fugue–   A kind of follow-the-leader piece. A melody is played and is followed by itself again and again.

Gamelan–	A percussion type instrument similar to a xylophone played in Java
Harmonium–	A small reed organ
Harpsichord–	A keyboard instrument which was popular during the 16th - 18th centuries, sometimes considered the "father" of the piano. However, the strings of the harpsichord are plucked by little quills, and the sound is not so loud as that of the piano.
Idée fixe–	A recurrent theme
Impressionism–	Music or art which suggests misty or hazy ideas rather than definite forms
Improvise–	Music which is composed while it is being performed or played
Incidental Music–	Music written as a background for a play or movie to set a mood
Jam–	Jazz term meaning to improvise on jazz music
Jazz–	Name given to a particular type of music credited to the black people. It was popular during the early twentieth century and was improvised
Leitmotif–	Short musical theme representing a certain character, place, idea or object
Librettist–	Person who writes the text or words of an opera, operetta, etc.
Libretto–	Words or text of an opera, operetta or musical, etc.
Licorice Stick–	Jazz term for a clarinet
Lyricist–	Someone who writes the words for a song
Mass–	A solemn service of the Roman Catholic Church. It has five musical parts.
Mazurka–	Polish folk dance
Minstrel Show–	Light entertainment in which white performers blackened their faces with burnt cork and sang songs, told jokes and danced
Minuet–	A popular dance during the Classical Period which followed a strict set of rules

Modernism–	New music written in the early twentieth century with harsh sounds, and crashing chords
Musical–	A musical play which combines a story, talking, singing, acting, dancing, costumes, scenery and an orchestra
Musicologist–	Someone who writes about music
Nationalism–	Love of one's country—in music, using native folk songs and dances as a basis for composition
Opera–	A play, usually entirely sung, with orchestral accompaniment, and scenery and costumes and acting
Operetta–	A light, usually humorous play set to music
Oratorio–	A biblical story set to music with solo voices and chorus and orchestra—no costumes or scenery or acting
Orchestra–	A group of musicians playing different musical instruments
Overture–	Music usually written as an introduction to a ballet, opera, operetta, oratorio or musical—sometimes an independent piece
Pitch–	The highness or lowness of a tone
Polonaise–	Stately Polish dance
Prelude–	An introductory piece of music
Prix de Rome–	A prize awarded to a student by the French government to study in Rome
Prodigy–	Unusual or extraordinary
Program Music–	Music which is connected to a story or an event
Psychedelic Rock–	Excessive volume, flashing lights, twisted pictures
Ragtime–	A popular musical relative to jazz, which is bright and happy and written with a definite form
Rhapsody–	Lovely, elaborate piece of music usually based on folk themes
Rock–	Music which began in the early '50s combining rhythm and blues and country western
Rockabilly–	Earliest type of rock begun by Elvis Presley

Romantic Period–	Period in history when all of the arts, particularly music, were more concerned with expressing feelings and emotions rather than following form
Scat Singing–	A kind of jazz vocal used when the singer invents nonsense phrases to go with the melody
Score–	Words and music of a musical show or a composite of all parts played by different instruments in a symphony orchestra. The conductor's score is arranged vertically on several staffs
Secular–	Non-religious music
Sitar–	An Indian stringed instrument with four to seven strings
Sonata–	A composition for one or more instruments written in three or four movements or sections
Song Cycle–	A record album with each song relating to the next
Song Plugger–	Pianist who plays songs of hopeful composers for music publishing companies
Soul Music–	Gospel style singing combining blues, jazz and rhythm
Sousaphone–	An instrument similar to a tuba which had it's shape changed by John Philip Sousa
Spinet–	A small keyboard instrument similar to a harpsichord
Spiritual–	A religious song telling a story and having strong rhythms
Syncopated–	Music with accents on normally weak or unaccented beats
Symphonic poem–	A piece of program music for orchestra suggesting a scene or creating a mood.
Symphony–	Large orchestral composition written in three or four movements
Tin Pan Alley–	Street in New York where publishing companies had piano players perform new music in the hopes of selling the new songs
Toccata–	A piece written for an instrument to let the performer "show off"
Waltz–	A lovely dance form with a 1, 2, 3 rhythm
Work Songs–	Songs sung by black people to help ease their burdens

Suggested Listening

LOUIS ARMSTRONG

Any jazz recordings which he has made
"Hello Dolly" from the show *Hello Dolly*

BACH

★*Toccata and Fugue in D. Minor*
Brandenburg Concertos (No. 2 & No. 4)
Cantata No. 147, "Jesu Joy of Man's Desiring"

BEATLES

★*Best of the Beatles*
1965, 1966, 1967, 1968, etc.
★*Sergent Pepper's Lonely Hearts Club Band*

BEETHOVEN

★*Piano Sonata in F minor, Op. 57, "Appassionata"*
★*Symphony No. 9 in D minor, last movement*
Symphony No. 3, No. 5, No. 6, No. 7
Piano Sonata in C sharp Op. 27, No. 2, "Moonlight"
Piano Concerto in E flat, No. 5, "Emporer Concerto"

BERLIN

★*"White Christmas"*
★*"Easter Parade"*
★*"God Bless America"*
Annie Get Your Gun
Call Me Madam

BERLIOZ

★*Symphonie Fantastique, 2nd movement*
Romeo and Juliet
Harold in Italy

BERNSTEIN

★*West Side Story*
★*On the Town*

BRAHMS

★*Academic Festival Overture*
★*"Brahm's Lullaby"*
Symphony No. 4 in E minor
Piano Quartet No. 1 in G minor

Compositions with stars were suggested in the text.

CHOPIN

★*Polonaise Militaire*
★*Opus 25, No. 9, "Butterfly Etude"*
Piano Music - any

COPLAND

★*Billy the Kid, "The Card Game," "The Fight"*
★*Appalachian Spring, "Celebration"*

DEBUSSY

★*Clair de Lune*
★*Afternoon of a Fawn*
La Mer
Piano Preludes

ELGAR

★The *Enigma* Variations
★*Pomp and Circumstance, March No. 1*
"Overture" Cockaigne, Op. 40

FOSTER

★Songs of Stephen Foster

GERSHWIN

★"Rhapsody in Blue"
★Selections from *Porgy and Bess*
American in Paris
Concerto in F for Piano
Songs of George Gershwin

GILBERT AND SULLIVAN

★*H.M.S. Pinafore, "Captain of the Pinafore"*
The Mikado
The Pirates of Penzance
Any of the Overtures

GRIEG

★Piano Concerto in A minor
★Selections from *Peer Gynt Suite,* "Morning", "In the Hall of the Mountain King"
Piano Music
Song of Norway - A Broadway Musical

HANDEL

★*Royal Fireworks Music,* Overture
Water Music Suite
Messiah, "He Shall Feed My Flock", "Hallelujah Chorus"

W. C. HANDY

★"Memphis Blues," "St. Louis Blues"
"Beale Street Blues"

HAYDN

★*Toy Symphony*, 1st movement
★*Symphony No. 94 in G*, 2nd movement, "Surprise Symphony"
Symphony No. 45 in F sharp (The Farewell)
Concerto in E Flat, for Trumpet and Orchestra

SCOTT JOPLIN

★"The Entertainer"
★"Maple Leaf Rag"
"The Cascades"
Selections from *Treemonisha*

LISZT

★*Les Preludes*
★*Liebestraume*
★*Hungarian Rhapsodies*
Variations on a Theme by Paganini
Piano Music
Piano Concertos No. 1 in E Flat and No. 2 in A

MENDELSSOHN

★*Fingal's Cave*, Overture
★*Capriccio Brilliant, Op. 22*
★*Midsummer Night's Dream*, "Wedding March"
"Songs Without Words"
Symphony No. 3 in A minor "Scotch"
Symphony No. 4 in A Major "Italian"

MOZART

★*Symphony No. 40 in G minor*, 3rd movement
★*Sonata in C*
Seranade "Eine Kleine Nachtmusik" K.V. 525
Magic Flute, Papageno's Song
Any piano concertos or sonatas

PROKOFIEV

★*Love of Three Oranges*, the March
★*Peter and the Wolf*
Piano Music
Ballet excerpts from Cinderella
Classical Symphony in D

RAVEL

★*Bolero*
La Valse
Pavana for a Dead Princess
★*Ma Mere L'Oye*
Piano Music

RIMSKY-KORSAKOV

★*Tsar Sultan*, "Flight of the Bumble Bee"
★*Scheherazade*, 1st movement
The Golden Cockerel

RODGERS AND HAMMERSTEIN

★*Oklahoma*
★*Carousel*
The King and I
South Pacific

SCHUBERT

★*Serenade*
★*Ave Maria*
★*Trout Quintet*, 4th movement
"The Linden Tree"
Any Songs

SCHUMANN

★*Scenes From Childhood*, "Traumerei" (Reverie), "Haschemann" (Playing Tag)
Piano Concerto in A minor
Waldscenen, Op. 82, "The Prophet Bird"

SIBELIUS

★*Finlandia*
Swan of Tuonela
Valse Triste

SOUSA

★"Semper Fidelis"
or other marches

STRAUSS

★*Tales of the Vienna Woods*
★*Blue Danube*

STRAVINSKY

★*Rite of Spring*, "Dance of the Adolescents"
Petrouchka
"Circus Polka"

TCHAIKOVSKY

★Selections from the *Nutcracker Suite*
★*1812 Overture*
Concerto No. 1 in B flat for Piano and Orchestra, Op. 23
Swan Lake Ballet
Marche Slav Op. 31
Sleeping Beauty Ballet

VERDI

★*La Traviata*, Act 1, scene 1
★*Aida*, "Grand March"
Selections from the operas *Rigoletto, Aida* or *Otello*
Il Trovatore, "The Anvil Chorus"

WAGNER

★*Meistersingers*, Overture
★*Lohengrin*, Prelude
Tannhauser, "The Processional"
The Valkyrie, "The Ride of the Valkyries"

Happy Listening!

Mrs. Kenneth Kennedy (Rosemary) is an alumna of Sweet Briar College and has done post graduate work at Tulane University. A native New Orleanian, and the mother of three, she has been involved in some form of music almost her entire life— either as a student, teacher, performer, listener or promoter. Along with active participation in sports, Mrs. Kennedy feels that both athletics and music have contributed much pleasure to her life and that the two transcend any geographical, political and language barriers which may exist.

Mrs. Roniger is a B.F.A. graduate of Newcomb College. She has taught art to children from age two to college age, specializing in encouraging children to experiment with a variety of materials. Because of her background in art education, Mrs. Roniger helped in planning many of the suggested activities for *Bach to Rock*. Mrs. Roniger has done illustrations and graphic design for various books and projects, but this was her first full length book with illustrations on every page.